THE BOOK MINE

THE PRINCE WHO BECAME A MONK
and Other Stories from Tamil Literature

M.L. Thangappa (1934) was born in Kurumbalapperi, Tirunelveli district, Tamil Nadu. Educated at St. John's College, Palayamkottai, he taught Tamil for over twenty-five years in the various colleges of the Puducherry Government until his retirement in 1994. He was on the editorial board of the Tamil monthly, *Thenmoli* (1962–67). He has published a number of books of poetry and essays in Tamil including *Adichuvadukal, Uyirppin Athirvukal, Ethu Valkai?* and *Nunmaiyai Nokki.* His translations from Tamil literature into English range from Sangam poetry and didactic poetry to the songs of Saint Ramalingam, Subramania Bharati and Bharatidasan. He has won the Bharatidasan Award (1991) of the Government of Tamil Nadu and the Sirpi Literary Award (2007) for lifetime achievement in poetry. Active in the Tamil language rights movement, he is also a founding member of the Puducherry Ecological Society.

Two of his translations from the Tamil classics have been published as Penguin Classics: *Love Stands Alone: Selections from Tamil Sangam Poetry* in 2010 and *Red Lilies and Frightened Birds* (a translation of Muttollayiram) in 2011. *Love Stands Alone* won the Sahitya Akademi award for the best translation of a regional work into English (2012). Thangappa lives with his family in Puducherry.

THE PRINCE WHO BECAME A MONK
and Other Stories from Tamil Literature

M.L. THANGAPPA

hachette
INDIA

First published in 2016 by Hachette India
(Registered name: Hachette Book Publishing India Pvt. Ltd)
An Hachette UK company
www.hachetteindia.com

SRD

ISBN 13: 978-93-5195-113-1

Hachette Book Publishing India Pvt Ltd
4th & 5th Floors, Corporate Centre
Plot No. 94, Sector 44; Gurgaon 122003, India

Typeset in Goudy Old Style 10.5/14.5 by
Manmohan Kumar, Delhi

Printed and bound in India by
Manipal Technologies Limited, Manipal

FSC
www.fsc.org
MIX
Paper from
responsible sources
FSC™ C104740

Contents

Introduction

Before you start, here's a fascinating fact – all the stories in this collection were originally poems! Tamil literature, just like literature from other regions of India, is full of stories written as poetry. These writings reflected the society, politics and culture of the time and place.

Historically, Tamilakam or the ancient Tamil country covered modern Tamil Nadu, Kerala and southern parts of Andhra Pradesh and Karnataka. The Sangam Age, from 300 BCE to 300 CE, is thought to be the richest and most important period of the literature of Tamilakam. It features the works and anthologies of many poets, dealing with many aspects of life, including social values, trade and war, among others. This was the period when the Tamil country was ruled by the three dynasties – the Cheras, Pandyas and the Cholas. People were at peace and could spend time on literary pursuits.

Unfortunately, much of Sangam literature has been lost. What is available has been divided into three broad categories based roughly on chronology. These are the Major Eighteen Anthology Series comprising the Eight Anthologies, the Ten Idylls, and the Five Great Epics. Tolkaappiyam, a commentary on grammar, phonetics, rhetoric and poetics is also from this period. It also includes classification of habitats, animals and plants as well as people and their behaviour!

Tamil legend goes that these were composed in three poetic assemblies or literary academies (called '*sangam*') held over twelve millennia ago on a continent (that later disappeared) to the south of India. This collection contains more than 2,000 poems composed by around 450 poets, of whom about 100 remain anonymous, and were brought together around 1000 CE. These Tamil poets were both men and women, coming from different professions and classes of society, and were judged as worthy and talented by their peers.

The poets had a unique relationship with the rulers of their land: the poets could pull up the kings if they did something wrong. Their respect had to be earned.

These poets sang of the bravery of their rulers. Sometimes, they acted as ambassadors for the kings and were tutors to the princes.

Some of their poems are about what is tangible (*puram*), such as sieges, everyday life, and so on. Others are about the heart, the feelings (*agam*). Every situation is described using themes, which have fixed times, landscapes, socio-economic situations and floral symbols. The idea was that human activities are affected by factors around them, and these factors were combined to create specific 'habitats' for poetry. For instance, land was categorized into five types: *kurinji* (mountainous regions), *mullai* (forests), *marutham* (agricultural lands), *neithal* (seashore) and *paalai* (wasteland). The imagery connected with these landscapes – flowers, trees, animals, birds, music, gods, weather, and so on – were used to communicate a particular mood connected with an aspect of life.

The three centuries after the Sangam Age saw an exchange between Tamil and Sanskrit – of words, concepts, ethics, philosophies and religious ideas. Around 300 CE, the Tamil country was under the Kalabhras, who were Buddhist, and a number of Buddhist and Jain authors wrote during this period, mainly on morality and ethics, grammar and lexicography.

The best known of these works on ethics in Tamil is the *Tirukkural* by Thiruvalluvar. This is a manual of ethics, polity and love, containing 1,330 couplets or *kural* divided into chapters of ten couplets each: the first thirty-eight on ethics, the next seventy on polity and the remainder on love. Other famous works of this period are *Kalavali*, *Nalatiyar*, *Inna Narpathu* and *Iniyavai Narpathu*. The Jain texts *Nalatiyar* and *Pazhamozhi Nanuru* each have 400 poems; each poem in the latter presents a proverb, illustrating it with a story.

At the beginning of the 4th century CE the Pallavas became rulers in the north of Tamil country, with Kanchipuram as their capital, and the dynasty reigned for over 500 years. The Pandyas ruled in the south. The early Pandya and the Pallava kings were followers of Buddhism and Jainism. In the middle of the 9th century the Cholas began one of India's most remarkable empires, in terms of administration and contribution to art and literature. Towards the end of the 13th century the Cholas were overthrown by the Later Pandyas, who ruled for about a century, and were followed by the Vijayanagara dynasty, whose greatest ruler was Krishnadeva Raya (1509-1529), and the Nayaks of Madurai and Thanjavur.

The early epics and moral literature, authored by Hindu, Jain and Buddhist authors, lasted up to the 5th century CE. From the 6th to 12th century CE, the Tamil devotional poems written by Nayanmars (sages of Saivism) and Alvars (sages of Vaishnavism) welcomed in the great Bhakti movement that later went across the entire Indian subcontinent. It is during this era that some of the greatest Tamil literary classics like *Kambaramayanam* and *Periya Puranam* were written and many poets were patronized by the imperial Chola and Pandya empires.

The Colonial Age began in the 17th century, when in 1639 the British East India Company established a trading post at the fishing village of Madraspatnam, now Chennai, the capital of Tamil Nadu. The later medieval period saw many small literary works and writings by Muslim and European authors.

I hope you will enjoy these small gems mined from the

great treasury of Tamil literature. Many such were lost in ancient times, and this is my effort to bring a few from those left to a wider audience.

M.L. Thangappa
Puducherry, 2016

1

Avvaiyar and the Highwayman

Avvaiyar was a great poetess in ancient Tamil country. She travelled constantly from one place to another, delighting kings, princes and the people with her verses. She did not, however, stay at one place for very long. All kings and princes of the Tamil-speaking world knew her well and she counselled them on many important matters.

Avvaiyar once went to meet Pari, the ruler of a small kingdom, with its palace atop a hill. Pari was, at the time, pre-occupied with the affairs of the state and did not have enough time for her. After a few days, Avvaiyar expressed her desire to leave.

'So soon?' Pari seemed surprised, and added, 'I haven't had the time to talk to you or listen to your poems. Please stay for a few more days and then I will be free to do that.' But Avvaiyar insisted on leaving and no amount of persuasion could stop her. Sadly, Pari gave in and ordered a large bag of gifts to be brought. He hung the bag on Avvaiyar's shoulder and bade her goodbye.

Avvaiyar stepped out of the fort with the heavy bag on her shoulder and descended the hill. After she had walked for an hour, she saw that the path led into a jungle. The bag was heavy and she was a little angry with Pari – he did not usually send her on foot when she had something to carry and always arranged for her transport. 'He is perhaps irritated with me for leaving when he did not want me to,' she thought.

Suddenly, there came the sound of horse's hooves. In a few seconds, a masked bandit appeared before Avvaiyar, blocking her path. He snatched the bag from her at sword-point, turned his horse around and disappeared into the forest.

Avvaiyar stood dazed and angry. A bandit in the land of Pari! Unbelievable! Pari was a very able ruler and zealously guarded his people from such ills. But here in broad daylight, she had been robbed of her possessions! It was not only a loss to her, but also an open affront to Pari. Avvaiyar decided that she would immediately report the matter to him.

Tracing her steps back vigorously, Avvaiyar reached Pari's fort, shocked and angry. Pari seemed surprised to see Avvaiyar back.

'What is the matter, Avvaiyar?' he asked. 'You were in such a hurry to go and now you are back!'

'Pari, I thought very highly of law and order in your kingdom,' Avvaiyar said breathlessly. 'But a bandit on horseback snatched the bag you had given me. It should never have happened in *your* kingdom. It is disgraceful; it is shocking.'

'I am very sorry that such a thing happened in my kingdom,'

said Pari. 'I will make sure the culprit is found. Meanwhile, please calm yourself and be seated. I will now compensate you for what you have lost.' So saying, Pari went inside and brought something on a silver platter. It was covered with a piece of cloth. He presented it to Avvaiyar and when the poetess removed the cloth, she saw the same bag that had been snatched away from her in the jungle! Avvaiyar could not believe her eyes. Was it possible that the robber had been caught so soon and the bag so quickly recovered?

Pari smiled at Avvaiyar, his eyes twinkling with mischief, 'You got your bag, now do you want to meet the robber?'

So saying, he put on a mask and the bandit stood in front of Avvaiyar!

'You must forgive me, Avvaiyar, for playing a trick on you,' he said quietly, removing the mask. 'I wanted you to stay with me a few more days. But you were bent upon leaving. I saw no other way to bring you back immediately. Are you upset with me?'

Words failed Avvaiyar. Her hands gently reached for Pari's while tears of tenderness trickled down her cheeks.

2

The Noble Heart of Athiyaman

Once during his wanderings over the highest mountains of his kingdom, Athiyaman, the famous king-chief of the Velir clan, noticed a *nelli* or *amla* tree growing in the crevice of a steep rock. It was of a special kind, yielding fruit once in twelve years. The fruit was believed to contain rare properties that prolonged the life of the eater. Access to the tree was difficult, for there were big boulders around, and the mere slip of a foot could send one hurtling down hundreds of metres into the valley.

Athiyaman climbed the boulders with great difficulty and reached the tree. He looked for the fruits, but there was only one. He climbed the tree, plucked the fruit and took it down with him very carefully. The fruit would give him a long life and he could enjoy the glory of his conquests for many more years.

Athiyaman returned to his palace with the fruit, but he did not eat it at once. After dinner and an hour of rest, he thought it was the proper time for him to eat the rare prize. He sat down to cut it, and just then his friend Avvaiyar came to see him.

Anyone who possessed such a rarity would have instinctively put it away to be eaten after the visitor left. Athiyaman, however, did not do that. The *nelli* fruit lay on the plate right in front of Avvaiyar. They were glad to see each other and talked of many things. While they were talking, Athiyaman casually pushed the plate in front of Avvaiyar. The poetess did not have the slightest idea of the rareness of the fruit or its wondrous qualities. She took it and ate it. Athiyaman waited till she had finished. Then he asked her how it tasted and she replied that it was very good!

Athiyaman said, 'I am very glad you came just now, or I would not have had the opportunity to offer that fruit to you.' Avvaiyar looked surprised and asked, 'Was that anything special?' Athiyaman smiled and told her all about it. The smile disappeared from Avvaiyar's lips. 'Oh, I feel very bad about this. Why didn't you tell me before I ate it?' She was bitter with remorse. Athiyaman smiled. 'If I had told you, you would not have eaten it, and I wouldn't have had the satisfaction of placing it in the right hands.' 'But did you not intend to eat it yourself?' asked Avvaiyar. 'Yes,' replied Athiyaman, 'but on seeing you, I changed my mind immediately. I decided to give it to you. Poets serve the world better than soldiers do.'

Avvaiyar was overwhelmed by Athiyaman's affection and magnanimity, and could not speak for some time. She took out her palm leaf and style, and wrote a poem then and there. It was a eulogy for Athiyaman and it celebrated the whole event in beautiful language. Athiyaman derived more delight from that poem than he would have had from eating the fruit.

Avvaiyar and Athiyaman are long dead and gone. Centuries have passed. But that poem of Avvaiyar still lives and through it, so does the greatness of Athiyaman. The *nelli* fruit gave Athiyaman a long life indeed!

3

Thondaiman and His Armoury

Athiyaman, the chieftain of Thagadur, was a formidable soldier. He had fought a number of powerful kings and emerged victorious in all the battles. His commanding power was such that even with a small army he was able to rout larger ones on many occasions. Even the three crowned kings of the Tamil country acknowledged his greatness and avoided confrontations with him.

One of Athiyaman's neighbouring kings was Thondaiman – inexperienced in warfare, but with very great ambitions. He desired to carve out a path of military glory for himself. He knew of Athiyaman's strengths, but thought that with a large army and excellent weapons Athiyaman's small army could be overpowered. So Thondaiman began to build up a large fighting force and a well-equipped armoury.

Athiyaman came to know of these military preparations of his neighbour. He knew very well that Thondaiman could not last a single day against him, and he did not like unnecessary bloodshed. He pitied Thondaiman and thought of discouraging him from his military adventurism. To avoid wounding Thondaiman's pride, he chose Avvaiyar the poet as his emissary instead of sending a diplomatic mission. Avvaiyar was loved and respected by all the Tamil kings. She could visit any of them any time and give them wise counsel without being thought of as an intruder.

Avvaiyar travelled to Thondaiman's kingdom and reached his castle. All along the way she racked her brains about how to fulfil her delicate mission without offending or provoking Thondaiman, but she could not think of a way of doing it. Thondaiman received Avvaiyar with great warmth. He entertained her well and gave a fine feast in her honour. They talked about many things, but Avvaiyar was unable to find an opening to carry out her mission.

After some time Thondaiman took Avvaiyar to his armoury. He had built it up over many years and was very fond of displaying it. It was indeed a very fine arsenal – a very impressive sight with a large quantity of dazzling, formidable weapons. All of them were arranged in neat rows. There were thousands of bows, arrows, spears, lances, javelins, swords, cutlasses, daggers, shields, clubs, coats of mail and more. They were of excellent steel and very fine workmanship – all newly made, well-oiled, highly polished and razor-sharp. Avvaiyar viewed them admiringly and in her mind she started comparing them with the oft-used weapons of Athiyaman. All of a sudden she saw her opportunity and knew what she would say to Thondaiman.

Pleased with himself, Thodaiman turned to Avvaiyar with great pride. 'What do you think of these weapons?' he asked. His voice was boastful and held a veiled challenge to Athiyaman.

Avvaiyar smiled. 'What a wonderful collection of arms!' she began. 'It is really very awe-inspiring to look at these newly-made weapons, oiled and polished and in fine array. I have never seen an armoury of this magnitude. Athiyaman's weapons are certainly no match for these. Having seen many a rugged battle, his weapons are blunted, bent or broken. Clashing with enemy weapons a hundred times, they have lost all their polish. Having maimed many an enemy soldier, they too have become disfigured. And they are not kept in orderly rows like this. Coming straight from a recent victorious battlefield, they lie scattered in the swordsmith's workshops, waiting to be mended and sharpened for the next encounter. They can never compare favourably with your fine-looking unused weapons.'

Avvaiyar said this as casually as possible, but Thondaiman caught her meaning. His boastful attitude vanished and he hung his head in silence. Avvaiyar's message had gone home.

4

Pari and the Jasmine Vines

Pari was one of the princes in the ancient land of the Tamil people. He ruled over the Parambu kingdom – a small territory surrounding the Parambu hill, on top of which he had his royal castle. Pari was not only a valiant soldier, but a man of great generosity. In fact, most of the Tamil kings and chieftains possessed generous qualities. Giving was considered the greatest virtue in those days. It was a shame to say no to anyone who asked for something. Minstrels and poets visited the courts of kings, sang beautiful songs and were rewarded richly, so that they might pursue their vocation without any worries.

Pari is listed by the poets as one of the seven great givers of ancient Tamil Nadu. He was very sensitive and full of love and concern for all living beings. The great nature-poet Kapilar was his friend. Avvaiyar the famous woman poet visited him very often. The courtyard of his palace was always crowded with poets and minstrels who came for rewards. They were welcomed most heartily and were treated to rich food and delicious drinks. Elephants and chariots were given away as presents. Pari moved amid them and hobnobbed with them all.

His land was fertile. Trees and shrubs grew all over the hill-country. The hill itself was dense with forests where jackfruits and mangoes abounded, edible roots grew wild and large beehives hung from trees. On the outskirts of the hill, *kanthal* (glory lily) and jasmine bloomed. The emerald green jasmine vines with their tiny white flowers, climbing and twining on the shrubs and trees, were a beautiful sight. The sweet fragrance of jasmine and other wild flowers filled the air in the evening and it was a joy to walk through the shady bowers on the mountain path. Pari loved those jasmines with great tenderness. He often walked amidst them and was carried away by their beauty and singular fragrance.

One day Pari was returning to his castle from a visit to the countryside. He himself was driving his royal chariot drawn by two splendid horses. The horses went up the mountain path in a trot and Pari was looking from side to side, admiring the wonderful mountainscape.

Suddenly his heart seemed to stop.

He had seen something that disturbed him. He pulled at the reins and stopped the horses, leapt from the chariot and hurried towards the thing that had disturbed him. It was a cluster of jasmine vines lying limp on the ground. Someone had hacked down and taken away the tree that had served as a support for the vines, without which the tender vines had dropped to the ground. A hot sun was beating down on them and they were wilting.

Pari could not bear the sight. How could he leave the fresh green vines there to wither and be trampled upon by passing cattle? He looked around. There was not a tree nor shrub within the reach of the vines. Then suddenly Pari's eyes caught sight of his own chariot and a tremor of joy passed through his heart. What an ideal support to the propless vines! Pari was jubilant. He walked towards the chariot, climbed on it and carefully drove it very close to the vines. He leapt down, took the vines one by one and entwined them round the four masts of the chariot and then spread them on the top. Soon, not a vine was left on the ground. The chariot was completely covered by the climbing stalks. It would support them thereafter. The jasmine vines would live and thrive.

Pari stepped a few yards back and viewed the vines as an artist would view his handiwork. He felt greatly satisfied. With a wonderful lightness of heart he unharnessed the horses and leapt on one of them. Leading the other by the rein, he trotted towards his castle.

5

Who Was He?

Many of the poets in the ancient Tamil land had different vocations. They wrote fine poetry but did not depend on it for their living. Some of them were small land-owners, some merchants and others were artisans. Still, there were a number of them who tried to live by only their poetry, and they were invariably poor. Of course, kings and chieftains patronized them and gave them riches and gifts, but the poets did not like to be with one patron for too long. So they wandered from place to place seeking new welcoming patrons. They never liked to pester unwilling chieftains.

Moreover, the poets had very generous hearts; they did not like to keep anything for themselves. The major portion of the wealth they received went to relatives and friends. Sometimes the relatives were so destitute that they came to live permanently with the poets. The poets never thought them burdensome, but took them under their care even though they themselves were not sure of a regular income.

Vanparanar was such a poet. Giving away everything he

received, he was invariably in want. And his poor relatives were always with him. Once he and his dependents set out on a long journey in search of patrons. Their path wound through rugged and barren country and they could not find food on the way. They travelled many days and at last reached a hilly region. The heat was terrible and they were overcome by hunger and fatigue. Unable to go further, they sought shelter under a large tree. They stretched themselves out on the ground in the shade and soon fell into a deep, tired sleep.

It was past noon. A stalwart figure of a man emerged from the jungle near where the party slept. The man was dressed like a hunter and carried bow and arrows. With fine features and a noble bearing, he wore a gold bracelet on his left arm and a string of sapphires round his neck. On his shoulder lay the carcass of a newly hunted deer. Noticing the weary figures sleeping under the tree, he went close and peered at their emaciated bodies and shrivelled faces. In a moment he understood the situation.

In the meanwhile, Vanparanar had woken up and tried to rise at the sight of the stranger. The hunter gestured to him to stay put. He laid down his bow, arrows and the dead body of the deer under the tree, and disappeared into the jungle.

Soon he returned with an armful of dry wood and twigs, threw them down, took up the deer and started skinning and dressing it with his dagger. By now the others had all woken up and they squatted round the stranger, watching the preparation of the meat with eager eyes. When the skinning and dressing was over, the hunter took out his flints and made a fire. He roasted the venison with professional skill and when it was nicely done, he cut it into large chunks and distributed them among the hungry men. The poet and his kinsfolk thanked him heartily and ate with great satisfaction. Next, the hunter guided them to a spring where they quenched their thirst.

Then he addressed the poet: 'I am glad you got something to eat. All of you look a little better now, but in this inhospitable jungle I cannot offer you anything more. However, I shall give you something as a token of my affection.' With these words he took off the string of sapphires from his neck and his bracelet of gold and put them into the hands of the poet. 'Kindly accept this as my humble gift,' he said.

The poet was dumbfounded. He could not find words to thank his benefactor. The hunter wished them well and turned to leave.

The poet addressed him, 'May I know whom we have had the good fortune of meeting? You have been very kind to us. We must remember you forever.'

The hunter smiled at him. 'Is it necessary?'

That was all he said and quickly walked away. After some time, the party resumed their journey. They met a hunting party on the way. The poet described the noble hunter and asked them if they knew who he was and where he lived.

One of them exclaimed, 'Don't you know him? He is Nalli, our leader and the chieftain of these hills – the Thotti hills.'

The poet was again overwhelmed. He had heard of Nalli and his benevolence. How he had longed to meet him! Now he had met him and not known him.

There was only one way the poet could remember him forever. And that is how he did it – in a fine poem.

6

Mosi Keeran and the King

The poet Keeran from the village of Mosi was known as Mosi Keeran. Once he wanted to see the Chera king Irumporai. The capital was a long way off from his village and he started on foot. When he reached the palace gates, he was very tired. The guards let him in, and after crossing a certain passage he came to a very quiet place. There in a side-room stood a beautiful couch with an inviting quilt of feathers on it. The poet sat on the couch to have a few moments' rest, but since he was exhausted he could not help lying down. He soon fell asleep.

This couch was not meant for anyone to sleep on! It was the ceremonial seat of the king's battle drum. Just like the royal sceptre, crown, the throne and the white parasol above it, the battle drum was an insignia of the king. It was a symbol of great honour and heroism. When a battle begins and the army marches towards the field, the battle drum – carried on the back of a caparisoned elephant – leads in the front. When the battle is over, the drum is given a ceremonial bath in the river and placed again on its seat with garlands and decoration. Occasionally, on ceremonial days too, the drum is taken to the river, bathed, decorated and brought back to the couch for rest.

It was on one such day, when the drum had been taken to the river, that Mosi Keeran had come and innocently dozed off on the vacant couch.

After some time, King Irumporai arrived there and noticed someone on the couch. Immediately his face flushed with anger – the person had defiled the sanctity of the couch by sleeping on it. His first reaction was to kill the offender, so he unsheathed his sword and hurried towards the couch. There he saw, to his surprise, not any country bumpkin as he had expected, but Mosi Keeran, the learned poet. His anger died down. Instead, he felt great tenderness towards the sleeping man. The poet must have travelled a long and weary way. Fatigue must have overcome him and without knowing what the bed was meant for he had slept in it. Full of tenderness, the king sheathed his sword, took a fan of peacock feathers from the bedside and started fanning the poet so that he might sleep still more comfortably.

How long he stood doing this kind service to the poet we do not know. When the poet awoke and looked up he saw the king fanning him. Shocked, he stood up at once, held fast the king's hands in protest, embraced him like a child and shed tears.

Later, when the king told the poet how it had all happened, the poet was again overwhelmed, and wept. He profusely apologized to the king for committing the sacrilege in ignorance, but the king had already forgotten it.

The whole chain of events is movingly described in a beautiful poem in which Mosi Keeran pays a fine tribute to the magnanimity of King Irumporai. The poem said that the esteem the Tamil poets enjoyed was due not to any innate greatness in them but because of their learning and their skilful language. The king's love for Tamil had saved the life of the poet.

7

Kanaikal Irumporai and the Race of Warriors

From very early times the chief evil among the Tamil kings and princes was fighting. They fought to display their valour and heroism. It was glorious to win and, if victory was not in sight, it was still a great honour to die fighting. If occasionally a king was defeated without being killed by the enemy, he killed himself before falling into the hands of his conqueror. The warrior clans considered it beneath their dignity to die in any way other than with a battle wound on the body. So obsessed were they with this idea of dying in battle that even if anyone died a natural death a deep sword-wound was inflicted on the body before it was disposed of. Even a stillborn child was no exception. This helped to keep up the honour of the warrior community.

Kanaikal Irumporai, the Chera king, belonged to that proud race of warriors. He fought fierce battles and had many victories to his credit. But at last in a battle with Killi, the Chola king, he was defeated, captured and thrown into prison.

Irumporai had been severely wounded in battle. He was terribly exhausted. His tongue was parched and his lips were cracking with dryness. He looked around for water but there was none in the prison cell. He gritted his teeth and tried to bear his thirst, but it was overwhelming. He asked the guards for water, but they were insolent fellows. Their prisoner had been a great king, enjoying all the luxuries of life, ordering people about. Now he was in captivity and they took pleasure in having him under their power. So they merely tossed a rude word at him and refused to give him any water. Deeply humiliated, the king seethed with anger, but what could he do, captured and chained as he was inside that narrow cell? His anger gave way to remorse. He sat shamefully and shed silent tears.

After a while, the surly voice of a guard aroused him and he was offered a mug of water. Without realizing what he was doing, he stood up and grabbed at the mug desperately. The next moment he remembered how he had been insulted, and his body shook in shame.

He stared at the mug in disgust. It was better to die than drink that water. Angrily, he threw the mug to the floor and buried his face in his hands.

After a few minutes, he lifted his head. He saw the broken pieces of the mug lying around him. He took a small sharp piece in his hand and pricked one of his fingers with it. With the blood that oozed out he wrote something on the prison wall. It was a poem that described his humiliation and the honourable practice in the family of dying with a battle-wound. He condemned himself most severely for accepting water from the guard and called himself the most shameless man in the world.

Finishing the poem, King Irumporai squatted on the floor, closed his eyes, drew a deep breath and held it in. It was a trick the proud Tamil warriors used to end their lives.

He never breathed again.

8

Ilaveliman and the Great Poet

Veliman was the head of a small principality in the Chola kingdom. He was generous to a fault and gave away the wealth of the palace to all those who sought his help, especially poets. Veliman had a younger brother called Ilaveliman who was just the opposite of Veliman in everything. He was stingy and did not like his brother's liberality to the poets. He hated poets from the bottom of his heart and whenever his brother opened up the treasury for them, his heart burnt.

Veliman died suddenly and Ilaveliman became the ruler. The first thing he did was to close the doors of the palace to the poets and minstrels.

Perunchithiran was one of the great poets of the day. He had been a friend of Veliman's and had enjoyed his hospitality and patronage many times. He lived in a faraway place and the news of Veliman's sudden death did not reach him. Great was his sorrow when he visited Veliman's palace and found Ilaveliman on the throne. When he stood before the new ruler, he was met coldly. Ilaveliman knew that the poet had been a good friend of his brother's but that was nothing to him. He eyed the man with contempt and just waved him to a seat on the side.

After some time, when the poet wanted to leave, Ilaveliman went in and asked a servant to send the poet away with a few gold coins. The servant took a few gold coins and offered them to Perunchithiran in a casual manner. He was deeply offended at this treatment meted out to him by Ilaveliman. However, he controlled his anger and, without touching the coins, rose and left the court abruptly.

From there the poet went to Kumanan, another generous patron of poets. Kumanan welcomed him with open arms. He delighted the king with his fine poems. After a few days, when Perunchithiran decided to leave, Kumanan showered him with riches and gifts. The bags of gold and the presents were so many that they had to be loaded upon the backs of two elephants. Elated and proud, the poet rode on one of the elephants, while the other elephant accompanied him.

On the way back lay the small principality of Ilaveliman. Perunchithiran, who was still seething from Ilaveliman's insult, wanted to have his revenge. In those days every king had a sacred tree as one of his tutelaries. The tree stood on an open field as the guardian spirit of the king and was watched over by soldiers. If an enemy could get past the guards and cause damage to the tree not only was it considered a great humiliation to the king but was also a way of throwing him a challenge. None but enemies who wanted a war took it up. So the sentries never dreamed anything untoward when

Perunchithiran, the friend of the former ruler, rode past them towards the tree.

In a flash the poet jumped off his elephant and, before the guards could understand what he was doing, tethered the elephant to the tree with the bags of gold and gifts still on its back. Then he mounted the other elephant, rode proudly towards the palace and demanded to see Ilaveliman. When a surprised Ilaveliman came out, the poet addressed him in bold and clear tones, and the words flowed out in the form of a poem, which said:

'O king, you were miserly and disrespectful, and failed to honour me properly. Do you think that without you, we poets would die? There are many worthy patrons in this land who know how to honour a poet. One such king has showered wonderful gifts upon me. He has loaded them on elephants and I have decided to give you one of those elephants with all the presents still on its back. Being niggardly with your wealth, I am sure you will be pleased to have them. And I have left the elephant tethered to the trunk of your sacred tree. Go and get it and stop being so niggardly.'

With these words the poet turned and rode away proudly, leaving Ilaveliman hanging his head in shame.

9

Nannan, the Cruel King

Perhaps in all the history of the early Tamil kings we read of, no one else is held in such poor esteem in the eyes of poets as Nannan. There is no record of his being bad in general or committing any unworthy act – except one heartless deed. He sent a young girl to her death for a flimsy reason. And for that he goes down in Tamil history as a villain no less despicable than Tarquin in the history of the Roman people.

The Tamil kings were fond of the symbols of their authority, power and honour. A tutelary tree or a tree of sanctity was one such symbol, and a king chose a tree of his own liking. Nannan chose a mango tree to be his special tree. It was large and it grew by the riverside. The king's soldiers guarded it day and night. If anyone would harm a single leaf of it, he would be guilty of sacrilege and liable to be put to death.

All the fruits the tree bore went to the palace; not even the guards were permitted to pluck and eat any. The soldiers did a daily count of all the mangoes, ripe and unripe, before they were satisfied that none of them was missing.

The tree had large branches overhanging the river. One day when the soldiers were not looking, one of the ripe mangoes fell into the river. Some distance down the river a young girl was bathing and the mango came floating to her. Quite naturally she picked it up and, tempted by its juicy flesh, bit into it with relish. She was enjoying the mango when the soldiers, finding a mango missing, came in search of it along the riverbank. Finding the half-eaten mango in the girl's hand, they arrested her and brought her to the king. He found her guilty and so according to the special law about the Tree of Sanctity he sentenced her to death.

Hearing this heartless sentence, crowds of people gathered at the palace. The girl's parents fell at the feet of the king and begged for mercy. Poets and elders of the city intervened on behalf of the girl. They said that the girl did not do it intentionally; she only took the mango from the river and that too without knowing that it was from the Tree of Sanctity. But all their arguments and entreaties fell on deaf ears. The king was adamant that the law be upheld. People could not reconcile themselves to this. In a final appeal to the king the girl's relatives promised to bring to him, in expiation, a life-size replica of the girl in solid gold. However, even that did not help in changing the king's mind.

Silence fell upon the court. With heavy hearts and tears, people left the court one by one, some of them openly cursing the king. There stood the unfortunate girl, trembling like a deer before a tiger, terror-stricken, forlorn and weeping. But the cruel king ordered her to be taken away and executed.

From that day onwards Nannan was looked upon by the people as a mean, cruel villain. Poets stopped singing praises of him. Many of his councillors stayed away from the court and some of them left the city to live elsewhere. Nannan went down in Tamil history as Nannan, the killer of a maiden.

10

Kumanan the Munificent

Kumanan ruled over the mountain-country of Mudirai. He was one of the seven great 'givers' eulogized by the poets because of his generosity. However, he had a brother called Amanan, who was just the opposite of Kumanan in every respect. Amanan was greedy for wealth and position and couldn't bear to see the riches of the palace being given to poets and mendicant minstrels.

So Amanan began to plot and plan against his brother. Kumanan came to know of this and could have easily crushed his brother if he had so wanted. But knowing Amanan's ambitions, he instead chose to abdicate. He went into exile and began to live as a hermit in the forest.

Amanan became the ruler. His hatred for poets was well known. One by one poets began to avoid his court and Amanan was happy.

Soon people began to speak openly of Kumanan's magnanimity

and the new king's niggardliness. Wherever Amanan's secret messengers went they brought back news of the people's love for Kumanan and hatred for their new king.

This deepened Amanan's anger towards his brother. He foolishly thought that if Kumanan were dead, people might stop talking highly of him and view Amanan in a favourable light. So he set a prize on his brother's head and announced that a thousand gold coins would be given to anyone who brought him Kumanan's head.

People were shocked, but no one paid any heed to the announcement. Kumanan was still so popular and loved that not a single person wanted to benefit by killing him.

Months passed.

One day a poet called Perunthalai Sathanar came to the land of Mudirai. He had heard of Kumanan's munificence but knew nothing of the latest developments in the country. When people told him what had happened, he was sad, but decided nonetheless to see Kumanan to pay him homage.

So he made his way to Kumanan's forest abode and told him of his poverty, of his hope of receiving gifts from Kumanan and his deep disappointment at the true king's exile. Kumanan was saddened. What a great welcome the poet would have received had he come during Kumanan's reign! Now he had nothing to give. Suddenly he remembered the price on his head and became overjoyed. He could still help a poet in want.

Without a word he drew his sword from its sheath and placed it in the hands of the poet. 'There is a price on my head,' Kumanan said. 'Cut it off and take it to my brother. He will give you a thousand gold coins.'

Sathanar was overwhelmed. He fell at Kumanan's feet and wept. 'Great indeed is your magnanimity, O King,' he cried, 'but how could you expect me to be so heartless as to take your life?' Kumanan lifted the poet up, but could say nothing to him.

For a minute there was silence between the two, but suddenly the poet had an idea. His face brightened. He wiped his tears and asked Kumanan to lend him his sword for a few days, after which he would come and return it. Kumanan readily gave him his sword.

A week later, Amanan was in his court when poet Sathanar appeared before him with Kumanan's sword in one hand and a severed head covered with a muslin cloth in the other. Blood was dripping from the sword and from the head as well. Everybody in the court was shocked.

The poet addressed Amanan, 'O King, you set a price on your brother's head – here it is. Give me the thousand gold coins.' Amanan had already recognized his brother's sword. Now the poet removed the covering and there was Kumanan's head dangling from the poet's hand. He told Amanan how selflessly the king himself had offered his head to be cut and taken to his brother. He started recounting the virtues of Kumanan when suddenly Amanan broke down and wept. The sight of his brother's severed head was too much for him. His hardness melted away and he was overcome with remorse. Unable to bear seeing the poet any longer he waved him away, fell on his knees before the head and begged forgiveness of his brother, 'You were magnanimous even in your death. How selfish I had become to cause your very death . . . Oh, I can have no forgiveness . . .'

'Take heart, O King,' said the poet. 'Your brother is not dead. He is alive and well. This head is merely a clever replica – come and take a close look at it.' Everyone in the court rushed for a closer look. It was indeed an identical copy of Kumanan's head, cleverly sculptured out of a soft material and painted to be lifelike!

A great shout of joy rent the ceiling of the court. 'Long live Kumanan,' the people shouted. Amanan's grief vanished but he was a changed man now. He confessed to all his past misdeeds and asked the people to forgive him. 'I will no more be king. Let us all go to the forest and bring back my brother to rule as before,' he said.

The poet Sathanar stood in a corner and wept tears of joy.

11

Karikal Valavan and the Farmers

Karikal Valavan was one of the most powerful Chola kings. When he was very young, enemies killed his father and threw Karikalan in prison. He spent all his early boyhood in enemy prisons, but he was such a clever and brave boy that he very cunningly escaped from the last one. With the help of his kinsfolk and friends he gathered a large army, routed all his enemies in a terrible battle and became king at a very tender age.

One day, in Karikalan's kingdom, a farmer was ploughing his newly purchased field when his ploughshare struck something hard. It was buried treasure – a large pot full of gold coins and precious stones. The farmer, who was very honest, thought that since he had bought the land only recently, he had no right to the treasure. Because in those days the state had no claim to such buried riches, he took the pot to the farmer who had sold the land to him. This man was not greedy either and he refused to accept the treasure, arguing that since he had sold away the land he had also forfeited his right to anything that lay buried in it. Since both were so scrupulous, each one insisted that the other keep the treasure. In the end they decided to present their case before their king.

The capital was a long way off. They walked on for days together and at last reached the palace. When they were ushered into the court hall they were surprised to find on the throne, not an old and sage king as they had supposed, but almost a boy. Glancing at each other sceptically, they paid their obeisance to the king, but instead of saying anything else they turned to leave the hall. The puzzled king called them back and asked them why they had come and why they were leaving without saying anything. The farmers hesitantly replied that they feared the young and inexperienced king might not be able to judge their difficult case.

The king was not offended. He smiled at them instead. 'All right,' he said, 'but you must not go without your case being decided. I have a very astute and elderly judge who will take a just decision. If you wait for a few minutes I shall send him to you.' So saying, Karikalan stepped down from the throne and walked away into the inner chambers of the palace.

Very soon an elderly judge entered the court. He occupied a seat next to the throne and looked benevolently at the farmers. He was very serene and looked learned, with grey hair and a flowing white beard. The farmers were satisfied and they now stated their case.

Sagacious as the judge was, he was not able to come to any decision. The arguments from both sides were flawless and neither side had the slightest advantage over the other. The judge suggested that they share the treasure equally between themselves, but the farmers would not agree to that. What could the judge do? The king could take the treasure away from them, but that would be stealing.

The elderly man racked his brains for a long time and then he found inspiration. He asked the farmers if they had sons or daughters of marriageable age. It so happened that one of them had a young daughter and the other a fine son. Very tactfully the judge suggested that a happy marriage alliance could be effected between the two families and the treasure given to the young couple as a wedding gift. The farmers saw that under the circumstances this was the best way out. They accepted the decision, thanked the judge and prepared to leave.

'Wait,' the judge said to them, and took his turban off. With the turban went the grey hair and when the judge ran his hand through his flowing beard, it came away in his hand as well! And there sat on the judge's seat none other than the young king himself, his eyes twinkling with mischief at the embarrassed farmers. The farmers knelt before the king and apologized for their earlier impertinence. The king laughed it away and sent them home with gifts.

12

The Telepathic Friendship

Pisir was a small village on the seacoast of the Pandyan kingdom. It was a beautiful village with the waves breaking on the rocky shore and the spray rising and falling like tiny little beads of glass. The village got its name from that; *pisir* means drops of water. In that village there lived a poet called Aandai. His name was a common one in those days and so this Aandai from Pisir was called Pisiraandai, and respectfully known as Pisiraandaiyar.

Pisiraandaiyar was a fine poet and a very high-minded gentleman. Even at an extremely ripe old age he looked quite young and his hair had not turned grey. People used to wonder at his youthful appearance and ask him how it was so. And Pisiraandaiyar gave them his answer in a poem.

'You ask me how I don't have grey hair even at this age. Well, I have never had to worry over anything in my life. My wife is a gem among women and my children are all virtuous.

My helpers seem to know my mind and are very prompt to do my bidding. The ruler of my country is righteous and just. Here, in my native village live men of great learning and exalted character, and they are my friends. Do you think I have anything to worry my head over?' Such was Pisiraandaiyar.

At that time in the Chola country there ruled a king called Kopperuncholan. He was a poet with a philosophic turn of mind. His noble qualities made him loved and respected not only in his kingdom but all over the three Tamil-speaking southern kingdoms – those of the Pandyas, the Cheras and the Cholas. Pisiraandaiyar and Kopperuncholan, being outstanding men of their times, heard about each other and knew they had like minds. They never met each other personally; yet they considered themselves friends and professed it openly to their other friends. They seemed to be connected in a telepathic relationship.

Being more a philosopher than a statesman, Kopperuncholan began to have trouble in the palace. There were intrigues against him in which his two sons were involved. The king was indignant at first and wanted to punish the villains, but he soon calmed down. He became tired of the whole affair and decided to renounce the kingdom in favour of his sons and lead a peaceful life of retreat. However, even after his abdication things happened that completely destroyed his peace of mind.

In those days it was a custom among the nobility that those who felt they had outlived their usefulness, ended their lives honourably by 'fasting unto death'. Such suicide was not looked upon as a crime or shame, but was viewed as a noble act by society since the reason for the act was honourable.

The person announced his intention and chose a quiet place, where he squatted on the ground facing north, and started his fast. When two or three persons happened to have the same intention they sat together. Their friends came to visit. They carried on normal conversations and even joked and laughed. As days elapsed, their strength wore out and in a couple of weeks they passed away.

Kopperuncholan announced his intention to go into his final fasting. Of course his friends and kinsfolk were sad but as it was the custom, no one tried to dissuade him. Some who were very close to him could not bear the thought of living without their good and righteous friend so they too decided to join him in the fasting.

When all of them sat down together and began their fast, Kopperuncholan had an intuition that Pisiraandaiyar, his unknown friend, might hear of his intention and come to join him. So he asked his other friends to keep some space reserved for Pisiraandaiyar in their midst. No one could believe that this would happen. Pisiraandaiyar lived in the faraway Pandyan kingdom and how could the news reach him so quickly? Even if it did, who would suppose that Pisiraandaiyar, just a friend from hearsay, would be in his mind and heart so closely connected with the king as to come and die with him? But Kopperuncholan seemed to be very certain. He told his companions, 'Just wait and see.'

The first day passed without event, and so did a couple more days. On the fourth day, about noon, the tired figure of a man was seen hurrying towards the fasting group. It was a total stranger but Kopperuncholan knew instantly that it was his friend Pisiraandaiyar. He rose from the ground and tottered towards the stranger. Pisiraandaiyar also rushed his steps and in a moment they were in each other's arms. They were very happy to meet for the first time and chatted enthusiastically. Kopperuncholan introduced Pisiraandaiyar proudly to his dumbfounded friends. The poet met them most cordially. Then as though he was aware of everything, he asked them which place was reserved for him. Kopperuncholan sat down and pointed to a place next to him. Pisiraandaiyar seated himself beside his friend and became one of the fasting group.

13

How Pothiyar Followed a King

As you read in the previous story, when Kopperuncholan started his fast unto death some of his friends wished to join him in sympathy. Pothiyar the poet was one of them. While the king accepted the company of old and spent men, he denied that privilege to Pothiyar because he was young and had been married only a few years. Moreover, his wife was expecting a baby. But Pothiyar, who had some sort of a spiritual relationship with the king, was very insistent.

So the king said, 'All right, but not now. Come after your wife bears you a son.' Looking cryptically at Pothiyar, he added, 'I will take you with me then.'

So Pothiyar had to go away. In a month or two, his wife had a baby boy. Meanwhile, Kopperuncholan had passed away, leaving Pothiyar in grief.

Usually in those days, when great men or heroes died, people erected monuments in their memory to pay them homage. Kopperuncholan also had such a memorial.

One day an aggrieved and forlorn Pothiyar came and stood before the shrine of the king. Tears ran down his cheeks. He recited a few poems in memory of his friend.

Suddenly, Pothiyar remembered the king saying, 'Come afterwards. I will take you with me then.'

'O friend, how will you take me with you now that you are a monument of stone?' he cried.

The story goes that at the poignant words of the poet, the monument of the king mysteriously cleaved open and to the bewilderment of all onlookers the poet gently walked into the crevice and vanished.

14

The Release of Ilanthathan

Once the Chola kingdom was divided and ruled by two princes of the same dynasty. Prince Nalankilli had his capital at Uraiyur while Nedunkilli ruled from Puhar.

Since each considered himself the rightful heir and the other a pretender, they were the bitterest of enemies. Each kept watching the moves of the other with suspicion.

Ilanthathan was a poet living in Puhar. He was a man of worthy character, but he was young and inexperienced in the ways of kings. So without taking into consideration the hostility between the two Chola princes, he travelled from Puhar and reached Uraiyur. For him it was just another Chola kingdom. But the king's guards, taking him for a secret agent, arrested him and brought him before the king. Hatred for his rival made the king blind. He supposed that the poet had been sent there on purpose to spy on him. The poet explained his innocent intentions, but the king would not believe him. He ordered the poet to be put to death.

The news reached Kovur Kilar, a senior poet and savant of Uraiyur. He was a person greatly revered by kings. Kovur Kilar did not know Ilanthathan personally, but felt that he was blameless. He knew that no genuine poet would involve himself in such politics of royal rivalry or agree to act as a spy. So he decided to save Ilanthathan from death at any cost and went to meet the king. As was wont in those days, he put all that he had to say in a poem and recited it before the king. The poem went somewhat like this:

'O king, don't you know the nature of poets? Just as the birds of heaven go in search of orchards, the poets go in search of patrons. No way is weary to them; no wilderness deters their will. Their tongues utter no unctuous words and in the songs they give their best. They are content with whatever they receive as gifts, which too they don't keep for themselves. Without a care for tomorrow they eat and drink, and without flinching they give. Such is a poet's harmless existence. And it is as dignified as the life of kings like you who are proud of conquest, power and sway.'

The king listened to the poem and knew on what mission the poet had called on him. He had such respect for Kovur Kilar and such faith in his words that he commanded that Ilanthathan be released immediately.

15

The Siege of Aavur

You read in the previous story how Kovur Kilar confronted the Chola king fearlessly for a noble cause. Many were the occasions on which the poet made such a brave effort.

King Nedunkilli, who tried to kill poet Ilanthathan, was not a very valiant king. He had ambitions for power and sovereignty over the whole of the Chola kingdom, but his courage often failed him. On one occasion when he occupied the fortress of Aavur, and prince Navalathan, the brother of his rival Nalankilli, laid siege, Nedunkilli did not have enough troops with him or the nerve to meet his enemy in battle. So he simply closed all the gates of the fortress and hid within.

Days passed. People inside the fortress began to suffer. All goods and supplies for them stopped. Since the siege began, all contact with the outside world had stopped. For a time they managed but soon the situation became unbearable. Hunger began to gnaw at them. Babies had no milk, for their mothers were starving. Even in rich homes, there was nothing to eat. The king's battle-elephants went without food. But king

Nedunkilli did nothing. He was neither prepared to fight nor willing to surrender.

Kovur Kilar came to know of the situation at Aavur. He was very sorry for the innocent people shut inside the fortress, so he decided to speak to the king on their behalf. As poets were held in great reverence by all, the besieging forces allowed Kovur Kilar to pass and he reached the fortress gates. He sent word to the king and was taken before him.

The poet spoke with frankness and courage, his words in the form of a poem. He spoke passionately of the hunger and misery of people locked up inside the fort. Then he reminded the king that he had no rightful claim to the fortress and must either give it up or fight it out with his rival.

'Either be a man of right or be a man of might,' said the poet. 'Being neither amounts to cowardice. And it is a shame on your part to keep hiding like this while people suffer.'

We do not know what actually happened after this. Hopefully, the king saw reason, renounced his claim to the fortress and sought peace with the besieger.

16

Malayaman's Children

Cholan Killivalavan had reason to be angry with Malayaman, the chieftain of Tirukovilur. He routed Malayaman's army and killed him in battle. Malayaman's children were captured alive and brought before the king. Killivalavan was so blinded by anger that he ordered the children to be trampled under the feet of an elephant.

The poet Kovur Kilar came to hear of this and at once hurried to the king's court. The king had already left to witness the execution of his enemy's children. Kovur Kilar rushed to the place. He saw the unfortunate, frightened children standing there with tears in their eyes. A bad-tempered elephant was being prepared to do the killing. The king sat in a corner, vengeful and waiting. The poet rushed to the king and entreated him to stop the killing in a poem:

'O great king, you descend from an illustrious dynasty of kings noted for their magnanimity. One of your ancestors was known to have sacrificed himself for the sake of a tiny pigeon. And he had on many other occasions relieved people of their sufferings. As for these children, humble as they are, they too come from a family that was very sensitive to the needs of poets, always ready to share what they had with them. Look at these guileless children, their sweet faces. Though they were scared at first, looking at the elephant they have stopped crying and stand watching it with childlike curiosity. How innocent they are, quite ignorant of the cruel fate that is awaiting them! But the crowd is surging around them, getting closer and closer, gaping at the children. This has terrified the children again. It looks as though they are going to cry. This is all I have to say. If you listen to me and act accordingly, it will be well; otherwise do what you like.'

The poet uttered these words with great vehemence and stepped away. The king took in everything and sat like a statue. He could not very easily bring himself to change his mind but he had to respect the wishes of a savant like Kovur Kilar. Going on with the execution would estrange him from the whole lot of poets and learned men in future and people would certainly begin to talk ill of him. Weighing all these things in his mind he relented at last and, though with hesitation, ordered the release of the children.

17

Pilambi and Avvaiyar

Kambar was the famous author of the Tamil version of the Ramayana. He was patronized by King Kulothungan III of the later Cholas. Being a genius and a poet of repute he was greatly respected in the king's court and nearly worshipped by the people. No wonder he was proud and always conscious of his greatness.

In those days people held poets in great reverence. They were looked upon as seers and prophets. It was considered auspicious to have their blessings. People of position and wealth sought to be sung by them. They believed that when a poet made a favourable mention of their name in a poem, it made them prosper. Moreover, through the poem their name became immortalized.

Kamban being famous, many people approached him and pestered him with requests to be featured in his poems. Conscious of his importance and perhaps to avoid being mobbed, he charged a fee of five hundred gold pieces for a mention.

Silambi was a court-dancer who craved to have her name mentioned in a poem. Being a modest woman, she was not wealthy, but still great was her desire to be sung by Kambar. She started saving money and in a few years saved up to two hundred and fifty gold pieces. She felt she could neither wait nor save any more and thought that being a court acquaintance for many years, Kambar would oblige her for half the fee. So she invited Kambar to her home one day, laid before him the 250 gold pieces and begged him to sing of her. Kambar was vexed but he did not show it. He collected his half-fee and started writing a poem on the outer wall of Silambi's house. Silambi was overwhelmed, but alas, her joy was short-lived. Kambar wrote just two lines of a four-line stanza and stopped. Moreover, there was no mention of Silambi's name in those lines. They celebrated the Chola king, the Chola land and the Chola rivers, and Silambi fell on her knees and begged the poet to put in at least one word about her in the poem. Kambar refused firmly, and pocketing the half-fee for the half-poem, he went away.

Great was Silambi's grief. Not only was she not mentioned in the poem, but all her savings were gone. And whenever she looked at the half-poem she smarted under the insult.

A few days passed. One morning, poet Avvaiyar happened to pass that way. (This Avvaiyar was different from the Avvaiyar mentioned in the earlier stories. The name Avvai was very common among Tamil women in those days and we have more than three women poets with the name.) Though a great poet, Avvaiyar was a very simple lady and her needs were but a few. Silambi met her in the street and invited her to her home.

Accepting the invitation Avvaiyar climbed on to the *pyal*, a raised platform on the side of the doorway, and sat there while Silambi ran into the house to prepare some food for her.

Avvaiyar looked at the wall casually and saw the half-poem there. Even as she sat thinking over it, Silambi returned and invited her into the house to eat. She was very apologetic that she had nothing to give Avvaiyar except thin *ragi* porridge, but Avvaiyar was very nice about it and ate with relish. Then the poet asked Silambi about the half-poem on the wall and Silambi sadly related the story behind it.

'So Kambar gave you half a poem for 250 gold pieces! I will furnish the other half for the nice porridge you have just given me.' So saying, Avvaiyar took a piece of charcoal, wrote two more lines and completed the poem. Reading those lines Silambi was overwhelmed with joy for she found herself well-complimented in them. With tears in her eyes she touched the feet of the poet with deep reverence and thanked her profusely. Avvaiyar blessed her and left.

The full poem ran like this:

'The monarch worthy of his name is Chola,
The land worthy of its name is the Chola land,
The river worthy of its name is Kaveri,
The woman worthy of her name is Silambi.
And the pair of anklets she wears on her lotus-feet
Are the only anklets worthy of their name.'

18

A Simile Worthy of a King

There lived in Sattimutram, a small village near Thanjavur in the Chola kingdom, a poet who was abjectly poor. He had a large family, but no regular means of income. He came to know that the Pandyan king in Madurai was a patron of poets and decided to go to Madurai to seek his fortune there. He set out on the long journey leaving his wife and children at home.

The poet travelled for many days and reached Madurai in a miserable state. It was very late in the evening and he knew no one in the large city. He could not go to the king's court at that late hour. He saw a rest house on a street corner and lay down on the open veranda. He was bone-weary, and hunger gnawed at the pit of his stomach. A chilly wind was blowing and he had no proper clothing to cover the upper part of his body.

Alone in the strange city, far away from home, hungry and cold, the poet became despondent. He thought of his unfortunate wife who would be suffering great ordeals during his absence. Moreover, she would be in terrible suspense not knowing whether he had reached Madurai or not. He wished he had someone who would carry her a message from him. Suddenly he thought of a pair of wood storks he had seen during the day by the side of a pond. They had been there for some time looking for fish and then they had taken off and headed north. He now imagined them flying over the Chola country and in the direction of his own village. His poetic imagination was kindled and a poem about his wretchedness took shape in his mind:

'Wood-stork with red-legs, your bill is coral-coloured and shaped like the tapering root-stock of the palm tree. If you go north with your mate, I would request you to go to Sattimutram, my village. You will find there a dilapidated house. Enter the house and meet my wife. She will be lying there staring at the ceiling, listening to the click of the gecko, hoping for some good omen. Tell her: "I met your poor husband in the Pandyan city. He was lying exposed to the wind without proper clothing, huddled up and covering his body with his arms and breathing heavily like a hissing snake." '

Having composed the whole poem in his mind, the poet began to recite it loudly, trying to forget his present situation and escaping into the excitement the poetry offered. Everything was silent at that midnight hour and his voice rang out loudly.

The Pandyan king, going on his nightly round in disguise, happened to hear the poem. When the comparison of the stork bill to the root-stock of the palm tree fell on his ears, he was swept off his feet. What a strange coincidence, he thought, for it was on that very morning that he had noticed storks and been intrigued by the singular beauty of their long, tapered bills. He had asked the court poets for an apt simile. There were so many comparisons, but nothing could surpass this.

The king was delighted and he wanted to know who the poet was, to shower him with riches. But he was in disguise and did not want to reveal himself. Moreover, he did not want to embarrass the poet by seeing him in his pitiful condition. So he withdrew from the place and went about his usual duty. When he returned after a few hours, the lean figure on the open veranda was fast asleep. The king took his regal shawl off his shoulders and spread it on the sleeping poet to protect him from the cold, and also to help the soldiers identify the poet later.

The poet woke up early in the morning and found himself covered with a rich shawl. While he sat there trying to guess who his benefactor might have been, the king's soldiers came, recognized the poet by the shawl and greeted him most kindly. They told him that the king wanted to see him. They dressed him in the fine clothes they had brought with them and with all respect took him to the king.

The king stepped down from his throne and received the unknown poet with open arms. He narrated the incident of the previous night to his surprised courtiers, repeating the simile. Everyone agreed that it was a fine, evocative simile, and were all praise for the poet. The king enquired about the poet's family and showered rich gifts upon him. He wished to enjoy the company of the poet for a few more days and so he sent all the gifts and gold to the poet's wife and children through his messengers with, of course, a joyous message from the poet.

19

Death Holds No Pain

The Pandyan king Poothapandian died at a very young age. His young queen Perunkopendu was beside herself with grief. She had loved her husband dearly and felt she could not live without him. She decided to immolate herself in the flames of the funeral pyre of her dead husband. In those days it was a common practice among devoted wives to end their lives in this manner, or to remain lifelong widows committing themselves to the memory of their spouses and subjecting themselves to all sorts of denials and austerities.

The grief-stricken Pandyan queen made her decision known to the elders and senior officials of the palace and asked them to make arrangements for her immolation. The elders were in a fix. They were not only sad that the young queen was going to die, but were also confronted with the problem of finding a ruler for the country. But they could not advise her against what she wanted to do. However, after discussing it between themselves, they at last made bold to approach the queen and request her to change her decision.

Great was the indignation of Perunkopendu at this strange request! She felt it was an insult to her to be asked to live on after her beloved husband's death. She was not afraid of death. Moreover, what was the nature of the life in store for her? Was she expected to live a life of wretchedness and misery as a widow? A widow was not even allowed to sleep on a soft bed. She had to lie down on the hard floor without even a mat on it. She could not eat any rich food – only cold rice and tasteless boiled greens without salt or condiments. It was indeed a life of humiliation. So she flew at the elders and rebuked them: 'You ought to know better, but you have all plotted against my happiness, you cruel men, asking me to live enduring all the indignities of widowhood. Why should I do that? After the death of my dear husband, his funeral pyre with the leaping tongues of flame appears as restful to me as the cool waters of a pond covered with blooming lilies.'

The elders could not answer. They stood with their heads bowed. Then in accordance with her wishes, room was made for her in the king's funeral pyre and Perunkopendu stepped into it.

20

War over a Poet

Irumporai, the Chera king, was a person of great learning and fine poetic gifts and his accomplishments were well known. Poykaiyar, a noble and accomplished poet, was his friend and tutor. They spent time together very often and enjoyed poetry.

The Chola kingdom lay nearby and Cholan Chengannan was its ruler. He too was a great warrior and a pursuer of military glory, but lacking in learning and devoid of poetic talent such as that of his neighbouring King Irumporai. Whenever people spoke highly of King Irumporai, Chengannan felt mortified. Proud as he was as a soldier, he felt small when he was amid learned men and poets. So he wanted to enhance his learning and write poetry like Irumporai. He consulted his ministers about this and they said that he must have the guidance of an able tutor. All of them agreed that Poykaiyar, the poet at the Chera court, was the most suitable person for this job.

King Chengannan sent a message to the Chera king telling him of his desire and requesting the services of poet Poykaiyar for a few years. Irumporai showed the letter to Poykaiyar. The poet felt that the Chola king's love of knowledge was not genuine, but motivated by vanity. He also felt that trying to teach how to write poetry to a person who had no natural gift for it was not worthwhile. Moreover, he did not want to leave the friendly atmosphere at the Chera court and the king's loving company. So he plainly told Irumporai that he was not at all willing to go to the Chola court and the king also did not try to persuade him. He sent a reply to Chengannan conveying the poet's unwillingness.

When Chengannan read the message he became enraged. He took it as an insult and his immediate impulse was to march against the Chera kingdom. However, he restrained himself and sent another letter. In it he said that unless the Chera king thought it fit to send the poet Poykaiyar to him within thirty days, the Chola army would march against the Chera country.

When this message reached Irumporai and Poykaiyar, they were sad. They did not want to plunge the country into an unnecessary war, but neither did they want to give in to the threat.

Thinking over it, Poykaiyar was even more convinced than before that he could never bring himself to teach such an arrogant warmonger. So they did not send any reply and started preparing for war. When the deadline passed, the Chola army attacked. The Chera army met the enemy forces outside the capital and a fierce battle ensued. Irumporai had his hopes on his mighty elephant force, but the Chola king had an excellent cavalry that struck like lightning. Frightened by the swift Chola horses, the elephants turned and fled, causing much devastation among their own forces.

Irumporai was defeated and taken prisoner. Poykaiyar was also captured. Both were taken to the Chola capital and thrown in prison.

In confinement, Poykaiyar was full of remorse for the Chera king. He felt bad that it was his obstinacy that had brought such troubles upon Irumporai and wanted to make amends for it. As a respected poet he knew that he would be able to meet the Chola king if he so desired and he thought of making use of the opportunity to seek the release of King Irumporai.

As Chengannan was fond of military glory, the poet knew that a poem celebrating his recent victory would greatly please him. Though it was against his principles to sing of war exploits, his sense of obligation and love for his king was so great that he decided to sacrifice his principles. And there seemed no other way to please the conqueror. So he started composing a poem celebrating Chengannan's victory, though actually the poem contained nothing more than a graphic description of the battle. When he finished the poem he asked to be taken to the Chola king and presented the poem to him.

Reading it, the king was pleased beyond measure. When he asked the poet what reward he wanted, Poykaiyar asked for the release and freedom of King Irumporai.

'You don't ask for your own release?' said the king.

'No!' replied the poet with dignity. 'My king is dearer to me than my freedom.'

The Chola king thought for a moment and then ordered that both the king and the poet be freed.

21

The Honour of a Family

In those days there were frequent wars among the Tamil kingdoms and every able-bodied young man had to be on the ready to fight for his king. Alertness meant cultivation of courage and rigorous training in the art of warfare. Thus a man's worth came to be measured by the bravery and heroism he displayed in the battlefield. Courage in battle was thought a great honour, and cowardice a shame. A coward turning tail in battle brought disgrace not only on himself but on his family as well. So mothers took pains to bring up their sons in courage and a sense of honour, and revelled in their exploits when they grew up and went to war. Victory, naturally, was a matter for great pride, but even in defeat a mother was proud of her son if he showed courage and died without giving up.

One such proud mother was an old woman with a wrinkled face and a withered body. She was the widow of a great soldier who had made his name in the battlefield. She had only one son, who was also a warrior fighting for the land he loved. She had brought him up as a brave soldier and was counting on him to continue the good name of the family.

The young man had gone to war and the mother was eagerly awaiting news from the battlefield. Soon, the news of victory came, but along with it came also the report of the death of the widow's son. In her jubilation over the victory of her country, she would have thought nothing of the death of her son, but it was rumoured that the young man had not been able to withstand fierce combat and had been killed with a spear in his back while fleeing the battlefield.

Great was her feeling of outrage when the old woman heard this story. Running away from battle was unheard of among Tamil soldiers. Even when defeat was certain they fell fighting or killed themselves. The old woman had instilled noble qualities in her son even when he was an infant, and now she could not believe her ears when she heard that he was killed while trying to escape death.

In her heart she felt that the story must be false, but she wanted to ascertain it. So in front of all the people who thronged to her house, she swore a terrible oath. 'Hear me, all who are here! I will go and find my son's body in the battlefield. If I find any injury on his back, surely he is unworthy to be called my son, and I will cut off these breasts that fed him.' So saying, she took the family sword in her hand and hurried away to the battlefield. And there, after a long search among the mangled bodies, she at last found her dead son. There he lay, as if he had fallen asleep, with a smile of contentment on his firm-set lips and a spear in his chest piercing right through his brave heart.

Great was her relief and joy when the old woman saw that. As she had believed, her son had died fighting, keeping the honour of the family intact. The rumour was false. Standing over the body, the old woman glowed with pride and experienced a joy that was even greater than what she had felt when she gave birth to him.

22

The Hasty Woman

Kovalan is a hero in the well-known Tamil epic Silappathikaram, in which many anecdotes highlight various glorious facets of his character. The following story describes his munificence and magnanimity.

In the city of Puhar, the capital of the Cholas, there lived a Brahmin and his wife. They were childless for many years and so they brought up a mongoose as a pet and showered all their affection on him. The mongoose was very attached to them, just like a child. After a few years a baby boy was born to them and they simply doted on him.

One day the husband was not at home and the wife had to go to the river to fetch water. The baby was sleeping in the cradle. There was no one in the house to look after the baby, but as he was asleep, she decided to go to the river nearby and return before the child woke up.

In her absence a large cobra descended down the ceiling, gliding along the rope of the cradle. He would have bitten the child but for the timely interception of the mongoose, which fought the cobra bravely and tore him to pieces. When he saw the woman of the house at a distance, he at once ran towards her to tell her of his victory. But the woman, looking at the blood-stained face of the mongoose, thought that the mongoose had killed her child. In her blind anger she threw the brass water pot at the mongoose and the poor animal was killed instantly.

The woman walked into the house and saw that the baby was sleeping calmly in the cradle. She then noticed the cobra lying dead, severed into pieces. It was then that she understood the loyalty of the mongoose and her own hasty foolishness. Full of remorse, she wept copiously.

When the husband came home and learnt about everything he was disgusted at his thoughtless wife. In those days it was considered a great wrong to kill pet animals. Also, it was believed that the sins of the wife would be visited on the husband. So, to be absolved of the sin, the husband decided to go on a pilgrimage to Varanasi, leaving his wife, as a punishment for her, to fend for herself.

The woman also desired to expiate her sins. She began a life of begging, to collect money for some charitable act. It was then that Kovalan saw her. Looking at her grief-stricken face he asked her what was wrong and she told him her sad tale. Kovalan took pity on her and gave her sufficient money to fulfil her vow. He also sent messengers after her husband, brought him back, advised him against abandoning his wife, settled them in a new home and provided them with all things necessary to last a lifetime.

23

Nanjil Valluvan's Gift

Nanjil was a hilly region ruled over by a chieftain called Valluvan. Once he had served as a commander in the Pandyan army, but later settled down to rule his small principality in a peaceful manner.

Once Avvaiyar, the well-known woman poet, and a party of women minstrels were passing through the Nanjil region. After a long journey they were tired and it was nearing noon. They camped in a shady grove and started cooking their lunch. Having cooked rice, they collected some edible wild greens from around the place and began to make a curry.

Someone suggested that a couple of handfuls of *thuvarai* gram (*toor* dal) would be nice to cook with the greens. But where would they get it?

'Why doesn't one of us go and ask the chieftain himself?' one of the women suggested. All of them agreed and Avvaiyar was considered the suitable person to go. So she went.

Seeing Avvaiyar, Valluvan was overjoyed. He received her with warmth and respect, and asked her what had brought her to his humble court. Avvaiyar told him of the camping party and of their immediate requirement. Valluvan was quite amused to hear such a small request coming from such a great poet. He was ready to fulfil it but felt that he would not be honouring Avvaiyar if he gave her only what she had asked for. Moreover, it would be beneath his dignity to send her away with just a little *thuvarai*.

He asked Avvaiyar to wait, and went inside. He ordered a large bag of *thuvarai* to be placed on the back of an elephant and the elephant was brought to the front yard. Then he went and told her that what she had asked for was ready. Avvaiyar saw nothing in his hand and was a little puzzled. Valluvan asked her to accompany him to where the cow elephant stood, loaded with a large sack.

Avvaiyar could not understand this and looked quizzically at Valluvan.

'Here is what you asked for – *thuvarai* – in that bag on the elephant's back. The elephant is yours too,' he said.

'A bagful of *thuvarai* with an elephant to carry it!' Avvaiyar could not believe her eyes or her ears. All this, for just asking for a handful of *thuvarai* to cook with the greens!

The poet was overwhelmed by the magnanimity of Valluvan. Then and there she composed and recited a poem in praise of Valluvan's noble act and after thanking him profusely rode away on the elephant with the big bag of *thuvarai* between her arms.

24

The Prince Who Became a Monk

It was the court of the Chera king. The king was seated on the royal throne, and his two fine sons were seated on either side of him. The day's proceedings were about to begin when the guard announced the arrival of a famous soothsayer.

The clairvoyant man entered the court and bowed to the king. Then his eyes fell on the two impressive-looking princes and were filled with great admiration. He looked at their faces for a few seconds, his eyes resting on one of them for a little longer. Then he turned to the king and, pointing to the prince seated to his left, said that he was the greater of the two princes and would one day become a remarkable ruler of the world. Hearing this, everyone was taken aback, for the prince he had pointed to was the younger of the two. It was the custom that the eldest prince inherited the throne from his father.

The king asked the soothsayer whether he was sure of his prediction. The soothsayer was certain. This upset the older prince even more. This prophecy had shocked him. He feared that his younger brother might usurp the throne, and this made him rather angry.

Meanwhile, the younger prince who was initially amused at the prediction, was watching the faces of his father and brother. Seeing their troubled faces he became sad. He himself had no intention of ever becoming a king, for his interests lay elsewhere. He had very fine poetic sensibilities and his ambition was to become a great poet. But he read his brother's thoughts, felt his jealousy and knew that thereafter there would be suspicion and mistrust in his brother's mind even though he might declare his intention to not become a king. He felt that if he remained in the palace any more, the relationship with his brother could never again be cordial. So he made a decision within himself then and there.

The younger prince stood up and proudly addressed the soothsayer: 'I don't think your prophecy is going to come true. For, this very moment I not only renounce my right to be a prince but also all worldly living. I shall become a monk'. So saying he took off his royal robe, his coronet and all the rich ornaments he was wearing. He drew his princely sword and cut off the beautiful locks of his hair. As the sword clanged to the floor, everyone watched him dumbfounded, and he walked majestically down the aisle and left the court.

However, the soothsayer was right in his foretelling, after all. The elder prince became the land's king all right, but the younger prince who became a monk later became a king of poets. He was the author of the famous Tamil epic *Silappathikaram*, among the greatest poets of the world and a remarkable ruler of the minds of people.

25

Shaped by Fate

One evening, the young Chola prince Nedumudikilli went for a walk in a grove near the seashore. There he met a beautiful woman who was a complete stranger to the city. The two young people stared at each other and fell in love immediately.

The girl refused to say who she was, but from that day onwards, they started meeting secretly. A month passed like this, but one evening the girl failed to turn up. The prince was deeply disappointed and he returned to the grove the next evening, only to be disappointed again. After a few days like this, the prince had the whole kingdom searched for his beloved, but there was not a trace of the girl.

The maiden was a princess from the distant Naga country, who had been visiting the Chola kingdom incognito. Owing to problems in her kingdom she had to leave suddenly without being able to inform the prince.

Returning home, she told everything to her father, the Naga king. The king already knew that something like this would befall his daughter, for years back when she was but a child, a soothsayer had predicted her future. He was not angry, therefore, but was worried about what he should do. Since she was the only heir to the throne she couldn't be sent back to the Chola prince to marry him and live with him.

In due course a child was born to the princess. It was a boy, and the princess felt that the right thing for her to do was to take care of the baby for a few months and then send him to his father, the Chola prince.

So after a few months of caring of the infant, the princess went in search of a merchant ship bound for the Chola country. She met a noble ship-owner and took him into confidence. Telling him her sad story, she placed the child in a fine casket of wood and entrusted him to the merchant to hand over to his father as soon as the ship reached the Chola port. The merchant accepted the responsibility and the princess returned home in peace.

Unfortunately, the ship carrying the child was wrecked off the Chola coast. In the confusion and havoc that ensued, the child was lost. The merchant tried his best to find the child, but was unable to. He himself somehow swam to the shore, clinging to a splintered board.

He went straight to the king – the prince had now become king – and reported everything with much remorse. The king received the news in great sorrow and ordered a thorough search of the seas, but the child could not be found. Heartbroken, the king neglected the affairs of the state and slowly the kingdom fell into disarray.

The casket in which the child was kept was designed in such a manner as to float in perfect safety on the waves should anything happen to the ship. Thus it travelled far and was washed ashore in another kingdom. It was taken to the king, who was overjoyed to find a child in it. Being childless, he adopted the child and named him Ilanthirayan, meaning 'young one who was borne on the waves.' Ilanthirayan later became a very famous king and founded the Thondamandala empire, a precursor of the Pallava Empire and one of the great empires of south India.

26

Outwitted by a Cowherd

There were at least three women poets in the Tamil land bearing the name Avvaiyar. They lived in different periods. The following story is told of an Avvaiyar who lived in the twelfth century.

It was a very hot day. Avvaiyar was travelling on foot in the countryside. The midday sun was beating down mercilessly upon her. Sweat ran down her forehead and cheeks. Overcome by fatigue, she looked around for some shade and hurried towards a large tree a little distance away. The tree was on the sandy bank of a lake, which was dry. A few buffaloes were lying under the tree.

As Avvaiyar drew closer to the tree she noticed that it was a *naaval* or *jamun* tree bearing edible berries. She also noticed a boy on the tree high up among the branches. He was plucking the berries and eating them with relish. Avvaiyar stood in the shade of the tree and looked up.

The boy, a bright-looking lad with a cowherd's staff in his hand, greeted Avvaiyar with a smile.

Avvaiyar smiled back and said, 'There seem to be a lot of berries on the tree.'

'Yes, and very nice ones, too,' the boy replied. 'Would you like to have some?'

Avvaiyar was already thirsty and hungry and the sight of the sweet-looking, dark-blue berries increased her need for some refreshment. She said, 'By all means, yes. Would you kindly get me some of those berries?'

'With pleasure,' the cowherd boy replied, adding, 'But I'd like to know first which kind of berries you want – the hot berries or the cold ones?' There was a twinkle in the boy's eyes.

Avvaiyar was puzzled. Was the boy trying to play a trick on her? She hesitated. She had never heard of berries being hot or cold. However, she did want the berries. To be on the safe side she said, 'Let me have the cold ones.'

'Are you sure you want only the cold berries?' The boy sounded rather mischievous.

'Yes, I do,' said Avvaiyar, though still uncertain about what he meant.

'All right, then,' the boy told her. 'I will pluck the cold berries and throw them to you, but you have to be careful in catching them.'

'Why don't you just shake the branch?' said Avvaiyar. 'That would be easier for you and I wouldn't have to pick them up off the ground.'

'Oh! Then all sorts of berries will fall down,' the boy said. 'You have to look for the cold ones yourself and pick them up.' So saying he took hold of one of the branches full of berries and shook it. The berries dropped to the ground in a copious shower.

Avvaiyar picked up the fully ripe berries, but she could not eat them straight away for they were covered with sand from the ground. She could not wipe the berries with her fingers since the flesh of the fruit was very tender and would come away in her hand. So she gently held each one of them in her fingers and blew off the sand before putting it in her mouth.

The lad watched her for a few seconds and then cried from the tree, 'Hey, grandma, you said you wanted only the cold berries, but now you are taking the hot ones! Be careful, lest they scald your tongue.'

Now the poet understood. When people had something very hot to eat they blew on it to make it cool. Blowing on the berries made them look hot! The learned poet felt a little ashamed at having been outwitted by the simple cowherd, but since it was a very enjoyable joke she complimented the boy on his cleverness and went her way.

27

Pari and the Three Crowned Princes

Pari was the ruler of Parambu, a small chiefdom within the Tamil country. We already know of his loving friendship with Avvaiyar and of his compassionate heart, which made him leave his royal chariot as a support to the jasmine vines. Though a ruler of a small kingdom consisting of only three hundred villages, he towered far above his contemporaries, surpassing them all in valour and magnanimity.

In those days, the Chera, Chola and Pandya kings were the three sovereign rulers of the Tamil country, and they alone had the right to wear crowns. However, there were many small states and principalities within those kingdoms, which enjoyed full independence so long as they did not disturb or provoke the crowned kings.

Pari was a fine soldier and a man of noble qualities. His fame spread far and wide. Poets sang highly of him, and minstrels and singers all over the Tamil land flocked to his court. This stirred up envy in the hearts of the three big kings.

Generally, the kings of the three Tamil dynasties were gracious and good, but there were exceptions too. The three contemporaries of Pari were such exceptions and they came together in their hatred towards Pari. They decided to get rid of him by defeating him in battle. They gathered a mighty army and marched against his kingdom, laying siege to the fortress on the Parambu hill, which was Pari's capital. The whole mountainous region was covered with that fortress and the area inside the fortress was fertile and self-supporting. The people did not need to get supplies from the outside. So, while the siege went on, the people inside the fortress were not bothered. With great confidence the soldiers of Pari defended their fortress.

Kapilar, one of the fine Tamil poets, lived in those days. He was a very close friend of Pari. He decided to meet the three kings in his private capacity as Pari's friend. He confronted the great kings with a poem:

'Do you think it is possible for you three to conquer Parambu so easily with all your drum-beating armies? Do not dream of it. For we will withstand your siege without much difficulty. We don't need any food from the outside. Our hills produce very good foodstuff without any farming. We have a variety of bamboo, growing wild all over the place, which yields a good crop of seeds. We have jackfruit in abundance. Sweet potatoes grow everywhere. And we have an abundant supply of honey from the giant-size honeycombs hanging from the cliffs. Our hills are vast as the sky and the springs thereof are myriad like the stars. You may have a large army of elephants and war-chariots, yet you cannot take our land by force, nor can you vanquish Pari in combat. But may I tell you how to win this land? Come like minstrels tuning your harps and singing his praises. Let your women accompany you dancing and beg for the land. He will give it away together with the hills.'

The three kings were mortified by the mockery in the poet's words. However, they could not do anything. They realized that their siege would never succeed. They withdrew their armies and went away in shame.

(The story goes that the envious kings who could not reconcile themselves to the greatness and fame of Pari plotted secretly against him and eventually killed him in a treacherous manner, thus sullying their own names.)

28

Ottakoothar and Pukalendi

Ottakoothar was the chief court poet of Kulothungan, the Chola king. When Kulothungan married the Pandyan princess, Pukalendi, a gifted poet from the Pandyan court was sent to the Chola court to act as a personal adviser to the princess who had become the Chola queen.

Pukalendi stayed at the court and with his brilliant wit and poetic talent began to enjoy great respect among the other poets. He also won much acclaim from the king. Ottakoothar did not like this and was envious of the new poet. Pukalendi was, of course, the greater of the two and this made Ottakoothar even angrier. There were frequent clashes of wit, poetry contests and heated arguments between them and Pukalendi always came out the winner.

And then it happened that Pukalendi wrote an epic poem.

In those days any new work of a poet was placed before an academy of learned poets and closely examined by them before it was approved. The author would read out his work and all the other poets would listen. They would question him on doubtful points, criticize him and draw attention to any serious flaw in the poem. The author could correct himself or offer his own explanations. Only when the examiners were satisfied fully was he allowed to proceed further.

Thus when Pukalendi began reading his poem, Ottakoothar had the chance of his lifetime. He disparaged him on every small point and refused to accept even the most reasonable explanations. Pukalendi knew that Ottakoothar was doing this out of ill-will and was irritated beyond measure. However, for all the malice he showed towards Pukalendi, Ottakoothar could not go against his own sensibilities. In fact, he was able to see the fine points in Pukalendi's work and secretly admired him. It was his own inability to write like Pukalendi that made him cynical.

One day it went beyond endurance for Pukalendi. In desperation he decided to put an end to his tormentor and regain his peace of mind. So on a dark night he went to Ottakoothar's house. He picked up a large piece of rock and managed to get into the house stealthily. Making his way into the bedroom, he hid himself behind a cupboard.

After some time Ottakoothar came there and lay down on the bed. He seemed tortured and was groaning uneasily. Pukalendi was waiting for him to doze off before he could smash his head. But within minutes, Ottakoothar's wife followed him into the bedroom, reprimanding him for not eating. Ottakoothar said that he had no appetite and that he did not want to be disturbed. She replied that she had special sweets for him to whet his appetite. Ottakoothar said that he was in no mood to eat sweets and that no amount of sweets would be even half as sweet to him as the poetry of Pukalendi.

Pukalendi, overhearing the conversation, was stunned at this unexpected compliment. He waited to hear more. Then Ottakoothar told his wife about the reading of Pukalendi's epic poem at the court and frankly admitted to her how greatly Pukalendi exceeded him in poetic talent and how he was wantonly criticizing him in court. Pukalendi gave up all intention of killing Ottakoothar. He emerged from his hiding place, greeted Ottakoothar with loving words and embraced him warmly.

Ottakoothar stood aghast. Pukalendi told him how he had come there with the intention of killing him. He begged Ottakoothar's forgiveness and expressed his sincere desire to become his friend. Ottakoothar also was moved by Pukalendi's words, and asked him in turn to pardon his despicable behaviour in court. They laughed at the ironic turn of events, forgave each other and from that moment became very good friends.

29

The Hand of the Peasant

Kambar the poet was banished from the court of the Chola king for an impertinent remark and he did not want to go back to his people. Having fallen from the grace of the king, he felt ashamed to face them. He thought it better to leave the Chola kingdom and seek adventure elsewhere. So he set out on a long and lonely journey. He had no money with him and he did not want to reveal his identity to anyone.

One morning, feeling terribly hungry, he spotted a small shop on the roadside. Kambar asked the shopkeeper for something to eat. The shopkeeper scowled at him and said that he would give nothing free before he made his first sale of the day. Kambar left him without saying anything.

After some time he came across an oil press worked by a pair of bullocks driven by an oil merchant. Oil was being pressed from the sesame seeds, and the residual matter that formed into a cake was being put aside. Kambar begged for a piece of that cake to satisfy his hunger, but the oil merchant refused to give him anything. Kambar walked away.

Not only was Kambar hungry, but he was also dying of thirst. He went and knocked at the door of a house that happened to belong to a Brahmin who came out and asked Kambar in a gruff voice what he wanted. Kambar asked for a drink of water. The Brahmin refused and waved him away.

Overwhelmed by hunger and thirst Kambar finally lay down under a shady tree. A peasant was ploughing his field nearby. It was nearing noon and the peasant's wife brought him his meal. The peasant squatted on the ground under the tree to eat. The food was nothing but cold rice soaked in water and a piece of pickle to go with it. Unable to bear the gnawing in the pit of his stomach Kambar shook off his shame and asked the peasant to give him a small portion of his food. The peasant asked Kambar to sit beside him and shared half of the cold rice with him. Kambar ate greedily and thanked the peasant for his kindness. He had never before eaten such humble food, but with the kind hospitality of the peasant it was as good as a royal feast to him. He wanted to honour the peasant with a poem, which he composed then and there and recited it to the overjoyed man:

'We shall never knock at the door
Of a shop-keeping merchant.
Nor shall we go to the door
Of the heartless oil-maker.
We shall never so much as glance
At a Brahmin's house.

The peasants are always there to help us.
The hand that grips the plough
Is the hand on which the kings depend.
It is the hand that holds
The wheel of charity.
It even sets aside fate.
It is the one that stands forever.
The hand of the peasant is the helping hand.'

30

Veli's Wall

During one of his wanderings, Kambar reached a village where a woman named Veli was living. Passing along her street, Kambar asked her if she had any work he could do. Veli asked him whether he could raise a wall in her backyard. Kambar agreed to do it.

Veli had had the wall built twice earlier, but it seemed there was an evil spirit in her garden which prevented it. So whenever the wall was built, the evil spirit caused it to fall. Kambar was the third person to be trying to accomplish the feat.

Kambar went to the backyard and started working. It took him a whole day to finish the job. When it was done, he turned away from the wall to go and ask for his wages. Suddenly the wall started shaking. Kambar guessed that an evil spirit must be behind the mischief. So he composed and recited a poem addressing the wall:

'I came here from the King's city
There is no one here
To appreciate my poetry
So I had to work with my hands
And raise you, O wall,
Have mercy on me
And stop falling at least
Till I have my wages
From this lady Veli
And leave this place.'

When the evil spirit heard Kambar reciting this poem, it realized his greatness, and decided to not bring the wall down. The wall stopped juddering. Kambar knew now that the wall was safe and went to get his wages. The lady took Kambar with her to inspect the wall. It stood intact. She thanked Kambar and gave him his wages, and he went his way.

31

Taming the Nasty Horse

Kongu country lies in the north-west part of the Tamil land. It is still famous for its stalwart men who love adventure. Once there was a young man called Kuppuchi in a Kongu village. He was an accomplished wrestler and well-versed in many other martial arts. He left his village in search of adventure and travelled north. Soon he reached the Telugu country and headed for the city of Vijayanagar. When he was about to enter the city gates, he was stopped by a knight. The sport-loving king had placed him there to challenge any newcomer to prove his strength against the king's wrestler. The knight wanted every stranger to kneel down before him before he entered the city. If someone did not want to kneel, he had to wrestle with the knight.

Kuppuchi did not want to kneel before the knight and so accepted the challenge. The knight was no match for Kuppuchi and was easily defeated. It was the first time that the knight had been defeated and people admired Kuppuchi for this. He proudly walked towards the palace. The news had already reached the king when Kuppuchi came to meet him. The king looked at Kuppuchi and liked him. However, he wanted to test his skill and cleverness in another sport.

The king had a nasty horse in his stables which never allowed anyone to ride him. He would wait patiently till the person saddled him and mounted. Then he would charge wildly, throw the rider off his back and trample him to death. If anyone succeeded in clinging to the saddle, he would straightaway make for the lake outside the city, plunge into the water and try to drown the rider. So far no one had succeeded in coming back alive from the encounter.

The king asked Kuppuchi to prove his mettle by taming this horse and riding him successfully. Kuppuchi asked to see the horse and was taken to the stable. He studied the horse for some time and said that he would accept the challenge. He would come back ready for the ride the next day and bring his own saddle. The king agreed.

The next day, Kuppuchi appeared before the king at the appointed time. The horse was brought there. Kuppuchi saddled the horse and jumped on him. The horse charged like a devil and tried to throw Kuppuchi off. Kuppuchi managed to cling to his back in spite of all his tricks. Unable to shake off the rider, the horse darted like an arrow and plunged into the lake. With the speed of lightning he tried to thrust the rider into the water. But the very next moment the horse neighed with pain and tried to rush out of the water. Kuppuchi did not allow him to do so and the horse screamed again and again. Then Kuppuchi gave the horse a free rein and both came out of the water. Something had happened to the horse. He became docile and readily obeyed every command of the rider. Kuppuchi rode thrice round the palace in triumph. The king was greatly impressed and he heaped a lot of gifts on the hero from the Tamil land.

What did Kuppuchi do to the horse? Hearing about the water trick of the horse, Kuppuchi had put a lot of quick-lime into the saddle. When water began to act on the quick-lime, it started to boil and produced a terrible heat. The horse could not endure the burning and tried to rush out of water. It was at that time that Kuppuchi became the master of the horse.

32

A King's Tribute

Mignili was a veteran soldier who served in the army of King Thithian. Once when the king was fighting a fierce battle, one of the horses in his chariot was killed by an enemy arrow and he did not know what to do. Mignili, who was fighting nearby, rushed to the aid of the king. He reined himself in the place of the fallen horse and started drawing the chariot forward, at the same time warding off enemy soldiers with one arm. This eventually led to the victory of King Thithian. The king was greatly pleased with the valiant and faithful Mignili and rewarded him well.

After some years, Mignili retired from the army and returned to his native village. He had lost his wife and had a daughter called Anni. She loved her father very dearly, for after the death of her mother he had brought her up lovingly.

Mignili owned a piece of land and a few cows. All day he worked in the field and in the evening he took his cows out to the pasture for grazing. One evening he was very tired and while his cows were grazing he sat under a tree, meaning to rest a while. But sleep made his eyelids heavy and he dozed off. One of his cows strayed into a neighbouring field and started eating the crops. Mignili was awake within a few minutes and he rushed to get his cow out of the field.

After some time, the owner of the field came there with his friends. He saw the damage done to his crops and was angry. He noticed the cows grazing in the pasture and came to enquire. Mignili, who was an honest man, admitted his mistake and promised to make good the loss.

However, the young man and his friends belonged to a particular clan that was not well-disposed towards Mignili. They surrounded him and assaulted him. Mignili, who still had his enormous strength, could have easily got the better of them all, but did not offer any resistance out of remorse. The wicked young men saw their chance and treated him most cruelly. They blinded him and ran away.

Soon it became dark and Mignili could not find his way home. He tied his blood-stained upper garment round the neck of one of the cows and sent it home. Anni, who was already anxious, saw the blood-stained clothing and rushed out in search of her father. She saw him lying under a tree, groaning with pain. With the help of some friends he was taken home. Anni took great care of her father and nursed him back to health, though his eyesight was completely lost. When he related what had happened, everyone was shocked and angry. Anni's indignation knew no bounds. She felt that the culprits should not go unpunished, so after a few days she went and reported the matter to the king.

The king was furious at what had happened to his beloved soldier. He did not want to wait till the culprits were brought to the court, so he himself rode to the village, taking Anni with him. He held his court under a tree and sentenced all the offenders to immediate death. When Mignili heard the news he came there, finding his way with a stick in his hand. Great was the sorrow and pity the king felt to see the great soldier walk like that. He embraced him and comforted him with kind words. Mignili invited the king to visit his home and the king readily agreed. Asking Anni to show the way, he took Mignili's hand in his. In spite of Mignili's protests, the king held on fast to his hand and led him gently home to the surprise of all the villagers.

It was a tribute the king paid to Mignili, who had drawn his chariot like a horse on the battlefield.

33

The Death Wish

King Meipporul was a devout worshipper of Lord Siva. He was such a fervent devotee that the very sight of a Saiva sage was enough to send him into raptures of piety, for such a person reminded him of the Lord Himself. He welcomed him with palms folded together in worship and awaited his biddings in supplication.

The kingdom of Meipporul was small and it was surrounded by several other kingdoms which were frequently at war with one another. Meipporul was a first-rate soldier and many were the neighbouring rulers who suffered defeat at his hands. King Muthanathan was one of them. He had repeatedly tried to subdue Meipporul and failed. Smarting under a series of crushing defeats, he decided to get rid of King Meipporul by any means, fair or foul.

One day there came a venerable-looking Shaivite sage to King Meipporul's palace. He had a flowing beard and matted hair that he wore like Lord Siva himself. He also had marks of sacred ash on his forehead, arms and chest. He was carrying a book-case in his hand, a cradle-like contraption to carry palm-leaf manuscript books. The sight of such an august sage stirred up pious feelings in King Meipporul's heart and he rushed out to the front yard to welcome him. He knelt before him and the sage gave him his blessings, saying that he had heard of the king's devotion and had come there to give him instruction in a recently discovered Saiva scripture.

The king was very pleased at this and took the sage into the palace respectfully. He was introduced to the queen and, when they got ready for the discourse, the holy man said that it was meant exclusively for the king.

The king led him to his private chamber. The king's bodyguard accompanied them, but the holy man looked at him disapprovingly. So the king ordered him to wait outside and went into the chamber alone with the sage and squatted at his feet, ready to receive the instruction.

The saint opened the book-case and pulled out a dagger. King Meipporul was a very alert soldier and could have easily defended himself against this impostor-sage who was none other than his arch-enemy Muthanathan in disguise. Muthanathan himself knew that fully well. He had come there not to take the king by surprise but to play upon his religious sensibility. He was right. King Meipporul did not want to hurt a person who was in the guise of a votary of Lord Siva. So with folded hands he sat there calmly while Muthanathan stabbed him fatally in the chest.

Meanwhile, the king's bodyguard, who had already suspected the sage to be an impostor, heard the king groan with pain and rushed into the room. Seeing the king lying in a pool of blood, he sprang at the impostor, drawing his sword.

'No! No!' the words flew from the lips of the dying king. 'Do not kill him. Whoever he is, he is in the image of my Lord. Not a hair of his should be touched. He should be safely escorted up to the border of our kingdom. See that no one does him any harm. This is not only my command, but my dying wish. Be a good servant and fulfil it.' Saying this, King Meipporul breathed his last.

Muthanathan, now deeply ashamed, was safely escorted outside the kingdom.

34

A Clever Rejoinder

In those days it was not an easy matter for poets to win recognition. Any major poetic work they had finished had to pass through a rigorous examination by a competent body of poets, and without their approval no book was considered to be of any worth. For this an author brought his book before this august assembly that usually met at a king's court. The poet read his poems aloud stanza by stanza while the other poets listened with great care and an ear for flaws. If they found any drawback either in thought, word or technique, they immediately pulled up the author. The author had to explain or be prepared to correct the defects, or the book would never gain appreciation. Usually the system worked well and no third-rate author was allowed to parade his half-baked composition as a wonderful piece of literature. However, human nature being what it is, some of the examining poets used this as an opportunity to snub their rivals.

When the poet Pukalendi was thus reading his book for approval, the poet Ottakoothar was part of the examining assembly. Pukalendi had been a rival of Ottakoothar for many years and the latter had always been envious of the former's gifts. Here was an opportunity for Ottakoothar to harass his rival and he listened with an unholy alertness, ready to raise an objection if he found a failing.

Pukalendi went on reading his epic. He reached a descriptive passage and read, 'It was a golden evening. The bees, drunk with honey, played music on the jasmine blooms. The jasmine bloom was a conch and the bee the conch-player.'

Ottakoothar stood up to voice his objection. 'Your image is wrong,' he said. 'A player of the conch puts the narrow end of the conch in his mouth and not the wider end. But the bee hums, sucking honey at the wider end of the flower. So the comparison is not apt.'

Pukalendi was in a daze for a moment. He knew that Ottakoothar was maliciously trying to find fault with him, for there was no need to take the imagery so literally. However, he either had to answer or admit his error before proceeding. Everyone was looking at him. In a moment he had a brainwave.

He said with a smile, 'Normally, a conch-player plays from the narrower end. But here, the bee is drunk. It does not know one end from the other and so has put its mouth on the wrong end.'

There was applause from the examiners. All along they knew that Ottakoothar was finding fault unnecessarily with a selfish purpose, but they had waited to see how Pukalendi would tackle him. And he had dealt with him successfully. They told Ottakoothar that they were satisfied with the explanation and that the author could go on.

Ottakoothar could do nothing but concede the point.

35

The Devoted Wife

Thiruvalluvar was the author of Thirukural, the world-famous didactic work in Tamil. Historically, nothing is known about him except that he wrote the book and that he was known by the name Valluvar to which the honorific 'Thiru' was later added. However, there are many legends about him that belong to a rich repertoire of Tamil tradition.

According to these legends, Thiruvalluvar had a wife called Vasuki who was very devoted to him. She is often held up to Tamil women as an example of an ideal and virtuous wife. She loved her husband dearly and obeyed him unquestioningly.

Someone who had heard about Vasuki's wonderful qualities wished to find out whether they were all true. He visited the home of Thiruvalluvar without revealing his intention. However, Thiruvalluvar read his mind and asked him to be his guest for a few days.

During one of those days Vasuki was drawing water from the well in the backyard and the guest was also in the garden doing something, all the while keeping a close watch on Vasuki, silently admiring the way she went about her work. Suddenly the voice of Thiruvalluvar came from the house calling out to Vasuki. She responded as if with the speed of lightning. She suspended the rope and bucket in mid-air and hurried into the house.

On another morning Vasuki served them cold rice for breakfast. Thiruvalluvar asked Vasuki to bring him a fan, saying the rice was steaming hot. Without so much as a puzzled look Vasuki went immediately and brought him a fan. That very day the guest departed, satisfied with what he had learnt.

Thiruvalluvar was a meticulous person and he lived a life of discipline. On the very first day of their married life, he had instructed Vasuki that before she served him food she should always place beside him an extra bowl of water and a needle. She did that throughout their life. But never once did Thiruvalluvar use the bowl and the needle and Vasuki did not know why her husband had wanted them there.

Years passed and Vasuki lay on her deathbed. Thiruvalluvar was sitting beside her, attending to her with loving care. Vasuki looked at him with something on her mind and her lips quivered. Thiruvalluvar understood that something was troubling her and that she was struggling to ask him a question.

He asked her to speak her mind freely. Then with much shyness Vasuki asked him about the bowl of water and the needle. Thiruvalluvar smiled. He said that if any rice spilled to the floor while she served him, he would pick up the rice with the needle and wash it in the bowl of water before eating. But never once had Vasuki spilled a single grain of rice while serving, and thus there had been no occasion to use the needle and the bowl of water.

Hearing this Vasuki was greatly relieved, for the question that had been troubling her all her life had finally been answered. She peacefully breathed her last.

36

Unequal Love

Ambikapathi was the son of the great poet Kambar. He was a good-looking young man and a talented poet himself. Kulothungan III was the Chola king at that time and Kambar was his poet laureate. Being Kambar's son, Ambikapathi visited the king's court often. His dazzling wit and charming manners attracted princess Amaravathi, the daughter of the king. They had frequent occasions to meet and by and by they fell in love with each other. But they had to keep their love a secret, for it was unthinkable for a princess to marry an ordinary man, even if he were the son of the poet laureate.

Days passed and the king came to hear of their relationship. He was indignant at Ambikapathi's audacity, but he wanted to be certain before he took any action.

Without revealing his suspicions to anyone, he arranged a banquet in the palace. Ambikapathi was invited. The king's intention was to observe Ambikapathi and Amaravathi himself to confirm his suspicion. When all the guests were seated princess Amaravathi walked into the hall. The moment

Ambikapathi saw her, he forgot the occasion and burst into a poem, paying tribute to the princess's beauty and charm. Kambar saw the danger and quickly changed the course of the poem by taking it up from Ambikapathi and ending it on a quite different note. Though his suspicions were strengthened, the king could not prove anything.

However, Ambikapathi and Amaravathi could not escape for long the watchful eyes of the king, and one day they were caught together. The immediate reaction of the king was to put Ambikapathi to death. But his counsellors advised him against it, saying that he might have to face the wrath of the common people if he dealt with Ambikapathi so summarily. So he called his council and put the matter before it. Kambar begged the king to forgive Ambikapathi. He assured the king that he would see to it that his son behaved himself in the future. Most members of the council were sympathetic towards Ambikapathi and some of them even boldly said that it was not wrong to fall in love.

Meanwhile, Amaravathi was in tears. She refused food and drink and pleaded with her father to not stand in the way of her happiness. She said that if anything happened to Ambikapathi, she would immediately kill herself. The king was in a dilemma. Ottakoothar, who was a poet and counsellor to the king and not very well disposed towards Kambar and his son, came up with an idea. He suggested that Ambikapathi should be put to a test. If he could extemporaneously compose a hundred stanzas of poetry purely on a devotional theme, without mixing in it a single thought or metaphor on love, he might be forgiven. But if he failed to complete the hundred stanzas or if any thought of love intruded anywhere in the stanzas, he should be put to death. The council agreed to this and Amaravathi was overjoyed. She had full confidence in Ambikapathi's poetic capabilities.

Ambikapathi, too, was sure he would win. His love for the princess would carry him through.

The test began. Ambikapathi was seated before the court. All the poet-judges sat on either side of the king. Amaravathi took her place on the balcony, hidden from Ambikapathi's eyes, but she could hear everything that passed in the court. She had with her one hundred roses with her to count out the stanzas as and when they were recited.

Ambikapathi started with an invocation to his favourite deity. Then he began the devotional series. It was child's play to him to rattle off stanza after brilliant stanza. Everyone was amazed at his extraordinary poetic prowess and many secretly wished that he should win. As he neared the end everyone was sure of his victory.

However, fate intervened at the last moment. When her hundred roses were counted out, a jubilant Amravathi stood up and applauded Ambikapathi. Seeing her, Ambikapathi discarded his devotional theme and began singing of her exquisite beauty, thinking that the test was over. But alas, the test was not yet over. There remained one more stanza to be completed.

In her ignorance Amaravathi had counted the stanzas right from the invocation. The time-honoured custom was to not count the invocation with the other stanzas. So the judges ruled that Ambikapathi had failed the test. Amaravathi's heart broke. She fell down in a faint.

Kambar again pleaded with the king for mercy. He pointed out that it was the fault of the princess, who had counted incorrectly. A few others supported Kambar, but the king would not listen. He was adamant that Ambikapathi should die and passed orders for his execution.

Ambikapathi was taken to the gallows and hanged. When Amaravathi came to hear of this, she fell to the floor again and rose no more.

37

Kambar's Revenge

After the death of Ambikapathi, who was his only son, Kambar left the court of Kulothungan in deep sorrow and bitterness. Rejecting all human company, he went into the forest and began to lead the life of a recluse. The heartlessness of the king rankled in his mind. He had been a very close friend of the king for many years, much respected and loved by the Tamil people as the greatest poet of his time. Yet the king had shown no consideration for his feelings. He had put Ambikapathi to death without a second thought. However hard he tried, Kambar couldn't forgive the king. He tried to immerse his grief in his writing.

Day in and day out he sat in his lonely hut in the forest and wrote poetry. One day while he was writing, there was a sound of running footsteps outside. He stopped and peeped out. A young man came running towards the hut. He was panting heavily and was at the point of breaking down. Kambar immediately recognized him as the Chola prince, the son of Kulothungan. The prince said that he was being chased by a killer elephant and begged Kambar to protect him. Kambar, whose heart was still full of rancour against the royal family, was overcome with hatred at the sight of the prince. The poet was holding a stylus in his hand and in an impulsive outburst of anger, he stabbed the helpless prince brutally.

The king was furious when the news reached him. He sent soldiers and had Kambar brought to him in chains. The poet faced him without flinching. 'You killed my son for no fault of his. Chance came my way and I killed your son, not for any fault of his, but to give you the same suffering and pain you gave me in my old age. I may be guilty in the eyes of the law, but not in the eyes of the world.'

Kulothungan sentenced Kambar to death. He said he himself would execute the sentence. Kambar said that he was ready to die then and there. The king took his bow and arrow. He aimed at the heart of the poet and drew the bow. The arrow pierced Kambar's heart. Gasping for breath, he uttered these last words:

'There are two kinds of weapons in this world. One is the arrow of steel and the other the arrow of words. The arrow of words is stronger and more dangerous than the arrow of steel. Your arrow of steel has killed me, but be sure my arrow of words will destroy not only you but the whole of your dynasty. My grief has so much power.'

With these words Kambar fell down dead.

{The Book Mine Gems}

THE PRINCE WHO BECAME A MONK
and Other Stories from Tamil Literature

Extra-special pages to help you know more about the characters in these stories . . .

THE WHO'S WHO OF KINGS AND POETS

AVVAIYAR

There were three important female poets with this name. Avvaiyar I lived during the Sangam Age and had cordial relations with the chieftains Pari and Athiyaman. She wrote 59 poems, of which most songs were related to Athiyaman and the rest to various aspects of state governance. Avvaiyar II lived during the Chola age. She was a contemporary of poets Kambar and Ottakoothar. She wrote poems mainly for children, both young and older, and all her poems impart basic wisdom related to everyday life. Not much is known about the third Avvaiyar.

PARI

He was a Tamil king who lived during the Sangam Age. He ruled Paramba Nadu and was famous for his generosity and patronage of art and literature. He is remembered as one of the last seven great patrons in Tamil literature. The poet Kapilar was his favourite poet and good friend. Pariyur or Parapuri near Gobichettipalayam in Tamil Nadu is named after Pari.

ATHIYAMAN

He was one of the rulers of the Sangam Age, and a patron and very good friend of poet Avvaiyar. He is remembered as a philanthropist, and described as a tough warrior in Avvaiyar's song 87:

Enemies! Take care,
when you enter the field of battle,
Among us is a warrior
who is like a chariot wheel,
Which made painstakingly by a carpenter
who tosses off eight chariots in a day,
Takes a month to shape!

THONDAIMAN

He was the ruler of Pudokkottai. Though not very experienced in warfare, he nonetheless had great ambitions, and an impressive armoury and large fighting force.

KAPILAR

He was a Tamil poet of the Sangam Age and a close friend and confidant of King Pari. He composed the most number of poems in the Sangam Age and wrote the *Kurincipattu* in order to explain the beauty of Tamil poetry to a north Indian king.

Kapilar was so deeply affected by Pari's death that he eventually starved himself to death.

VANPARANAR

He was a poet belonging to the Sangam Age, and the first Tamil poet to record nearly all the historical events that happened during his lifetime. He used similes or narration to explain anecdotes in his poems. He described four famous battles of Tamil Nadu – at Venni, Vagai, Kudal and Pazi, and also wrote of great Tamil kings and bad practices in the Tamil society.

MOSI KEERAN

The poet Keeran from the village of Mosi was known as Mosi Keeran. He believed that the poets were held in high esteem not because they were great, but because of the skilful way in which they used the Tamil language.

NALLI

He was the leader and chieftain of the Thotti Hills. Known for his benevolence, Nalli once cooked a meal for, and gave his jewels to, a destitute poet and his relatives.

Kanaikal Irumporai

A brave and proud warrior, he is remembered as one of the great Chera rulers. He died in captivity, by starving himself to death.

Ilaveliman

He was the head of a small province in the Chola kingdom, and brother of the kind, benevolent Veliman. Ilaveliman was stingy and held a strong dislike for poets, and was taught humility by the poet Perunchithiran.

Perunchithiran

He was a great Tamil poet of his time and enjoyed the friendship and patronage of King Veliman. He was instrumental in teaching the miserly Ilaveliman humility.

Nannan

He ruled the part of Kerala called Poozi Nadu and is remembered as a notorious king because he had a young girl executed. The incident is written about in *Kurunthokai*, poem 292.

KUMANAN

He ruled Madurai during the Sangam Age and was more inclined towards poetry than war. He encouraged and patronized all forms of art. Kumanan was one of the seven great 'givers' eulogized by the poets because of his generosity.

PERUNTHALAI SATHANAR

A poet from the Sangam Age, he taught the miserly Amanan the error of his ways by making him realize the value of his kind brother, King Kumanan.

KARIKAL VALAVAN

One of the most powerful Chola kings, he ascended the throne at a very young age. One of the oldest water-regulator structures in the world still in use today, the Kallanai, was built by him.

PISIRAANDAIYAR

The greatest Tamil poet of his time, Pisiraandaiyar lived in the Pandyan kingdom. He joined King Kopperuncholan in his death, even though they had never met before. The story of their friendship lives on even today.

KOPPERUNCHOLAN

He was a famous ruler of the Chola country. Patron and friend of many poets of his age, he was a poet himself, and wrote a few poems in the *Kurunthokai* collection and in *Purananuru*.

POTHIYAR

A poet of the Chola period, he wanted to die along with his friend King Kopperuncholan, but was refused because he was too young. He eventually followed his beloved king when the deceased king's monument mysteriously parted and took him in.

NALANKILLI AND NEDUNKILLI

They were two princes who ruled a divided Chola kingdom, with Nalankilli ruling from Uraiyur and Nedunkilli ruling from Puhar. The two were at constant war with each other until the death of Nedunkilli. Nalankilli is written about in fourteen poems in *Purananuru*.

ILANTHATHAN

He was a poet living in Puhar, under the rule of Prince Nedunkilli. Mistaken to be a spy, he was imprisoned when he travelled to

Nedunkilli's rival Nalankilli's land. Nalankilli later released the poet at the request of poet Kovur Kilar.

Kovur Kilar

A respected poet, Kovur Kilar lived in Uraiyur. He got Ilanthathan released from captivity and also advised, and succeeded, in stopping Nedunkilli and Nalankilli from self-destructive fighting. He also stopped the assassination of two young children by the Chola king Killivalavan.

Killivalavan

A Chola king celebrated in eighteen songs, Killivalavan was himself the author of a poem. He was brave, benevolent and headstrong and was dissuaded, by Kovur Kilar, from getting his enemy's young children killed.

Kambar

He is the famous author of the *Ramavataram*, the Tamil version of the Ramayana, which has more than 10,000 stanzas. He was patronized by King Kulothungan III and held in high esteem by kings and citizens alike.

KULOTHUNGAN III

He was a ruler of the Chola empire, who strengthened and brought order to a weak Chola kingdom. The king contributed significantly to Tamil architecture, and patronized the great Tamil poet, Kambar.

SILAMBI

A dancer in the Chola court, she yearned to have a poem written about her by poet Kambar, but did not have sufficient money to pay him. She was eventually written about by poet Avvaiyar, where the poet praises her for her generosity and kindness.

PERUNKOPENDU

The exemplary wife of Pandyan king Poothapandian. After the death of her husband, she too stepped into his funeral pyre.

POYKAIYAR

Friend and tutor to Chera king Irumporai, he refused to teach poetry to the Chola king Chengannan. However, he finally wrote a poem in praise of Chengannan to get Irumporai released from captivity.

CHENGANNAN

A Chola king, he was a great warrior and distinguished military strategist. He also desired to learn the art of poetry.

KOVALAN

The hero in the famous Tamil epic *Silappathikaram*, Kovalan was known for his generosity.

VALLUVAN

The chieftain of the hilly region of Nanjil, Valluvan was earlier a commander in the Pandyan army. He was known for his magnanimity. When asked for a little *thuvarai* (dal) by the poet Avvaiyar, he gave it to her along with an elephant.

NEDUMUDIKILLI

He was a Chola prince who fell in love with a Naga princess and fathered Ilanthirayan, who was a famous king and founder of the Thondamandala empire.

OTTAKOOTHAR

He was a Tamil court poet to three early Chola kings, including Kulothungan. A part of the Saivism literary movement, he wrote poems for kings and also contributed devotional poems to Tamil literature by writing the *Saraswati Andhadhi*, in praise of the goddess Saraswati.

PUKALENDI

A witty and talented poet from the Pandyan court, Pukalendi was the personal adviser to the Chola queen. He won much acclaim at the court of the Chola king Kulothungan. He was at odds with the poet Ottakoothar, but the two became good friends later.

MIGNILI

A veteran soldier who served in the army of King Thithian, Mignili drew the king's chariot like a horse during a battle after the king's horse was killed, which eventually led to the victory of Thithian.

THITHIAN

A just and valiant ruler, the king never forgot that Mignili drew his chariot like a horse during battle. Later, when Mignili was blinded by some men, the king himself rode to the area and sentenced them to death.

MEIPPORUL

The chieftain of Miladu Nadu, he was a devout worshipper of Lord Siva. He was murdered by Muthanathan, the king of a neighbouring state, who came disguised as a Saiva sage. Meipporul, however, commanded that the imposter not be harmed.

MUTHANATHAN

He murdered King Meipporul in the guise of a Saiva sage, because he knew that Meipporul would never harm a sage.

THIRUVALLUVAR

A famous Tamil poet and philosopher, he wrote the *Thirukural*, a work on ethics. He lived sometime between the 3rd century BCE and the 1st century BCE. He had an exemplary wife, who was completely devoted to him.

AMBIKAPATHI

The son of renowned poet Kambar, Ambikapathi was a talented poet himself. He fell in love with King Kulothungan's daughter and was eventually put to death because of it.